A MAN
WITHOUT DOUBT

BY DENVER C. SNUFFER, JR.

Published in the United States by Mill Creek Press.
Mill Creek Press is a registered trademark of Mill Creek Press, LLC.
www.millcreekpress.com

ISBN-0-9891503-7-2
ISBN-978-0-9891503-7-8

Printed in the United States of America on acid-free paper.

First Edition: June 27, 2016.

Cover design by David Christenson. The cover art includes part of a lithograph created in 1852 illustrating the martyrdom of Joseph Smith (printed by Nagal & Weingaertner, New York. It is based on a drawing of G.W. Fasel which was converted into a lithograph by C. G. Crehen). The cover artwork is discussed at the end of this book.

In memory of the Apostle Paul:

Are they ministers of Christ? (I speak as a
fool) I am more; in labours more abundant,
in stripes above measure, in prisons more
frequent, in deaths oft. Of the Jews five times
received I forty stripes save one. Thrice was
I beaten with rods, once was I stoned, thrice I
suffered shipwreck, a night and a day I have
been in the deep; In journeyings often, in perils
of waters, in perils of robbers, in perils by mine
own countrymen, in perils by the heathen, in
perils in the city, in perils in the wilderness, in
perils in the sea, in perils among false brethren;
In weariness and painfulness, in watchings
often, in hunger and thirst, in fasting often, in
cold and nakedness. Beside those things that
are without, that which cometh upon me daily,
the care of all the churches. Who is weak, and I
am not weak? who is offended, and I burn
not? If I must needs glory, I will glory of the
things which concern mine infirmities. The
God and Father of our Lord Jesus Christ,
which is blessed for evermore, knoweth that I
lie not.

The Apostle Paul writing to the Saints at Corinth; 2 Cor. 11:23-31.

TABLE OF CONTENTS:

Introduction:
Are They Ministers of Christ...I am More
-Page 1-

Power In The Priesthood:
...In Labors More Abundant
-Page 9-

Lectures on Faith
By Joseph Smith
...The Care of All the Churches
-Page 35-

Kirtland Collapse/Missouri Peril:
...In Perils Among False Brethren
-Page 83-

Joseph Smith History
By Joseph Smith
...In Watchings Often
-Page 99-

A Missouri Dungeon:
...In Prisons More Frequent
-Page 121-

Joseph's Letter from Liberty:
...In Perils By My Own Countrymen
-Page 133-

Conclusion:
...I lie not
-Page 155-

Glossary
-Page 165-

INTRODUCTION:
ARE THEY MINISTERS OF CHRIST?
...I AM MORE

Every Christian should be acquainted with Joseph Smith. Although unnoticed by most Christians, his life and message transcend denominational divisions and speak to us all.

Joseph Smith was born in obscurity the day after the Winter Solstice of 1805. The ebb and flow of daylight was more significant to an agrarian society than it is today. The date he was born would have been recognized by farmers as the day on which the light grew in nature. It would prove symbolic, foretelling something of his life.

He died thirty-eight-and-a-half years later in a hail of gunfire. He left Illinois to escape mob violence on the summer solstice of 1844. At the behest of friends he returned across the Mississippi River to surrender to the Illinois authorities the day after the solstice. Four days later, as sunlight began its decline, he was slain. The alignment between growing and receding daylight and Joseph's life may be no accident.

He claimed to be God's Prophet. That claim put an end to obscurity, attracted followers and critics. His claim was ultimately what provoked the hail of gunfire that ended his ministry and life. He was doubted and believed. In spite of that, he was a man without any doubt about his Divine calling.

Joseph Smith said an angel predicted his name would be "both good and evil spoken of." That has proven to be true. As the founder of Mormonism, Joseph has been vilified and praised. More than eighty-four different religious sects claim him as their founder. The Church of Jesus Christ of Latter-day Saints, headquartered in Salt Lake City, Utah, is the largest and most recognized. Today is it more a financial institution than religious body, paying scant attention to anything Joseph Smith actually taught. In this book the Salt Lake sect is referred to as the "LDS church" or "LDS Mormonism."

American scholar Harold Bloom wrote about Joseph:

> I ... do not find it possible to doubt that Joseph Smith was an authentic prophet. Where in all of American history can we find his match? In proportion to his importance and his complexity, Joseph Smith remains the least-studied personage, of an undiminished vitality, in our entire national saga.... If there is already in place any authentic version of the American Religion then, as Tolstoy surmised, it must be Mormonism, whose future as yet may prove decisive for the nation, and for more than this nation alone. (*The American Religion: The Emergence of the Post-Christian Nation* (New York: Simon and Schuster, 1992), pp. 95, 97.)

His significance is unappreciated because Christians have never seriously considered him as an independent Christian figure. Thus far it has been impossible for Joseph Smith to be divorced from institutional Mormon claims, and therefore he has been relegated to a neglected footnote for most Christians. It is time for him to emerge into view, un-eclipsed by the corrupt and self-serving institutions of Mormonism. Freed from the claims of institutional ownership, he has something to add for every Christian.

On September 4, 1843, the *New York Times* wrote:

> This Joe Smith must be set down as an extraordinary character, a prophet hero, as Carlyle might call him. He is one of the great

men of his age, and in future history will rank with those who, in one way or another, have stamped their impress strongly upon society. It is no small thing, in the blaze of this nineteenth century, to give to men a new revelation, found a new religion, establish new forms of worship, to build a city with new laws, institutions, and orders of architecture, to establish ecclesiastical, civil, and military jurisdiction, found colleges, send out missionaries, and make proselytes on two hemispheres. Yet, all this has been done by Joe Smith, and that against every sort of opposition, ridicule and persecution. In the short space of fifteen years, Joseph Smith, unschooled in the learning and the methods of the world, did all these important things. How was it possible? Does not the only rational explanation lie in the claim that he was God-taught[?]

Mormons present an image of Joseph Smith designed only to fortify their claim that they are a new, heaven-established franchise that alone offers mankind salvation. They tie their claims to Joseph Smith, despite the fact that all of the Mormon sects have strayed far from Joseph's form of Christian religion.

This book will tell the events leading to Joseph Smith's three greatest failures and then provide his written responses to each of them. Fortunately, he had something important to say after each set-back. To understand his response, it is important to know the circumstances in which he wrote. Despite abandonment by one-time followers, and universal condemnation from contemporary Christian churchmen, he never doubted God spoke to him and had a work for him to do. In 1829 God's voice warned him about trusting the wrong people: "[Y]ou cannot always judge the righteous, or …you cannot always tell the wicked from the righteous[.]" (*Doctrine and Covenants* 10:37—referred to as "D&C.") This proved to be a troubling weakness throughout his life and contributed to his murder. Trusted insiders turned on him. Their proximity to him lent credibility to their accusations. They conspired to attack, imprison and ultimately kill him.

The three ordeals discussed in this book were caused by the treachery of disaffected Mormons. That does not suggest there were not loyal Mormons. There were thousands of loyal, decent and even noble adherents of Joseph's preaching. They are not the focus of this book.

I write this as an excommunicated Latter-day Saint. Studying and writing about Mormon history cost me membership in The Church of Jesus Christ of Latter-day Saints (LDS church). I am not a Mormon apologist. Mormon history reveals the deep flaws of the LDS church, and there is little reason for even its devoted members to ignore them. The flaws of LDS Mormonism are perhaps less serious than the many other denominations claiming Joseph Smith as their founder, but all of them are so different today that Joseph Smith would hardly accept any of them as a faith he founded. His last dream or vision anticipated this would happen. The night before he was murdered he dreamt his farm was overtaken by neglect, weeds and brambles. As he considered how to remove the curse and desolation he saw before him, a company of furious men confronted him and ordered him to leave. He initially protested claiming the farm was his, which provoked fury and threats against him. The mob claimed the farm was theirs and not his. In the dream he relented, telling the men, "I had no desire to live upon it in its present state." (*TPJS*, p. 393.) Joseph Smith would have little desire to be affiliated with Mormonism in its present state.

Introduction

This book is not addressed to Mormons, nor will it either support or oppose the claims of the various Mormon sects. This is an attempt to explain Joseph Smith apart from institutions. This book will not attempt to "convert" anyone or initiate anyone into an organization. The Mormonism of Joseph Smith no longer exists in any institution.

I will set the historical stage so he can explain himself in his own words. Whether one believes in angels, gold plates written by ancient inhabitants of the Americas, the restoration of an ancient order, or a modern revival of a Biblical prophet who could declare, "thus saith the Lord," there is no reason to question whether Joseph Smith believed such things. He never waivered, and was ultimately slain because of his beliefs. There is no requirement to believe his bold claims in order to benefit from his story.

This book will cover three critical episodes from his life. In the first, he was on a years-long failing quest to obtain and distribute Divine priesthood to others. (See "Melchizedek Priesthood" in Glossary.) The failure did not discourage his quest. It caused him to reflect on the failure, and then work to overcome and succeed. He responded by producing *Lectures on Faith*, a series of lectures designed to instruct others on what faith is and how to develop faith in Christ.

His second failing campaign was an attempt to establish a community of equals to be called "Zion." That failure resulted in a loss of followers and accusations of sedition against the United States and treason against the state of Missouri. There were mob attacks that destroyed Mormon settlements, Mormons slaughter by the Missouri State Militia, and an order of exile in 1838 by Governor Lilburn Boggs removing all church members from Missouri.

Prior to the Missouri expulsion, church historian, John Whitmer, who at that point was disaffected with Joseph and the church, absconded with the church's history. Many church leaders left, denouncing both him and Mormonism. Joseph immediately responded by composing a replacement history, now known as *The Joseph Smith History*. It was written in the months following the collapse of Zion, and at a time of Mormon upheaval.

The third failure came when he was arrested, imprisoned, and condemned to die for treason against the State of Missouri. While in prison, he composed a letter to his followers. That letter is the third and final document of his that is reprinted in this book.

This book examines these three watershed moments in Joseph's life that were the impetus for the three important Christian compositions he authored. Those three writings reveal his heart and mind, and in turn allow us to make an assessment of his beliefs. His responses to the trials do not read like a great defeat, nor are they words of mourning for what had been lost. They are hopeful, optimistic and full of faith in God. The optimism of his words should not mask the bitter setting in which they were composed. A better measure of Joseph can be taken by his own words than the words others have used to describe and explain him. His written responses to these bitter ordeals are full of Christian faith, hope and charity.

Joseph Smith was audacious. But his audacity arose from something critics have largely ignored. Whether anyone else thought he was chosen by God to restore the original Gospel of Jesus Christ, Joseph was driven with confidence that defied any setback or defeat. If he was deluded, his delusion failed to produce self-doubt. He doubted only his capacity to teach faith in Christ to others. There has not been so audacious a character on the Christian stage since the Apostle Paul. Like Paul, Joseph Smith was "born out of due time." (1 Cor. 15:8.) His preaching produced conflict with traditional Christianity as Paul's preaching did with Peter. (Gal. 2:7-11.)

Introduction

Will the time ever come when Christians will cease disputing among themselves by claiming to be "of Paul" (Protestant), "of Cephas" (Catholic), "of Christ" (Evangelical), (1 Cor. 1:11-13) or "of Joseph" (Mormon)? Are we doomed to continue the cycle of breaking apart the "Body of Christ?"

POWER IN THE PRIESTHOOD: IN LABORS MORE ABUNDANT

Joseph Smith was born in Vermont as Thomas Jefferson was beginning his second term as US President. The Smith family later moved to upstate New York while the Second Great Awakening was in its heyday. It was a time of religious revivalism, affecting all of western New York. Revivals by religious rivals riled the residents so effectively it earned the reproach "the burned over district."

His family, like most at the time, were indecisive believers in Protestantism. Smith family members belonged to Methodist, Presbyterian and Baptist churches. Like many others in their quest to connect with God, they mingled folk magic with their Christianity.

Joseph had only a limited education, and as was common at this time, his reading skills were designed to acquaint him with the *Bible*. In the spring of 1820, during the religious fervor of the burned over district, Joseph declared he had been visited by God the Father and Jesus Christ. His first account of their visit focused on personal conversion and individual salvation from sin. Years later, his account evolved to describe cosmic significance for the salvation of all mankind. His account shifted to reflect a change in his understanding of his role from a converted believer, forgiven of his individual sins by an act of the Almighty, into God's prophet, voicing warnings to the world. Believers heard the voice of God through Joseph. Critics heard megalomania.

Joseph Smith's claims do not lend themselves to neutrality. He is regarded as either a true prophet or false prophet. Some think him both: a true prophet who fell from grace. Whatever the decision, he certainly left some remarkable material from which to judge and categorize him. This book is designed to allow the reader to hear his voice before deciding how to judge him.

In the fall of 1823, he claimed again to have a heavenly visitation. This time, by an angel who helped to inscribe the *Book of Mormon* on gold plates. The angel ultimately entrusted those plates to Joseph Smith. He translated them into English, then borrowed money to publish the text in 1830.

In 1830, he also founded and became the president of a church based on the *Book of Mormon*, and called it the Church of Christ.

Joseph taught his followers one standard, but then managed them using another. Although he paid lip service to the idea every man must approach God directly, he managed the church contrary to that concept. As the leader of the church, he micromanaged, provided too many answers, and was too quick to dictate yet another "thus saith the Lord" revelation to govern its members. Two years before he was killed, he realized his followers had been crippled in their relationship to God, and *he* was the source of their problem. In 1842, he scolded his followers by telling them "that they were depending on the Prophet, hence were darkened in their minds, in consequence of neglecting the duties devolving upon themselves, envious towards the innocent, while they afflict the virtuous with their shafts of envy." (*Teachings of the Prophet Joseph Smith*, ("TPJS") p. 237-238.) It was too late. The habit had developed over a dozen years and he would be dead within two years of that sermon. Those left behind would be habituated to follow the direction of a central authority figure. Although Mormonism fractured, and continues to fracture today, almost all splinter groups submit to the control of a single, central president. Joseph's failure was apparent to him by 1842, but escapes notice in the splintered world of Mormonism.

One of man's most important and difficult duties is to develop faith in God. The final writer in the *Book of Mormon* (Moroni), recorded:

> [H]ave angels ceased to appear unto the children of men? Or has he withheld the power of the Holy Ghost from them? Or will he, so long as time shall last, or the earth shall stand, or there shall be one man upon the face thereof to be saved? Behold I say unto you, Nay; for it is by faith that miracles are wrought; and it is by faith that angels appear and minister unto men; wherefore, if these things have ceased wo be unto the children of men, for it is because of unbelief, and all is vain. For no man can be saved, according to the words of Christ, save they shall have faith in his name; wherefore, if these things have ceased, then has faith ceased also; and awful is the state of man, for they are as though there had been no redemption made. (Moroni 7:36-38.)

The idea that faith is necessarily accompanied by spiritual gifts was also the view of Methodist founder John Wesley. In his eighty-ninth sermon, *The More Excellent Way*, Wesley taught,

> It does not appear that these extraordinary gifts of the Holy Ghost were common in the church for more than two or three centuries We seldom hear of them after that fatal period when the Emperor Constantine called himself a Christian, and from a vain imagination of promoting the Christian cause thereby heaped riches, and power, and honour, upon the

Christians in general; but in particular upon the Christian clergy. From this time they almost totally ceased; very few instances of the kind were found. The cause of this was not (as has been vulgarly supposed) "because there was no more occasion for them," because all the world was become Christian. This is a miserable mistake; not a twentieth part of it was then nominally Christian. The real cause was, "the love of many," almost of all Christians, so called, was "waxed cold." The Christians had no more of the Spirit of Christ than the other Heathens. The Son of Man, when he came to examine his Church, could hardly "find faith upon earth." This was the real cause why the extraordinary gifts of the Holy Ghost were no longer to be found in the Christian Church— because the Christians were turned Heathens again, and had only a dead form left.

Like Wesley a half-century earlier, Joseph Smith faced the Christian dilemma: how can man develop faith in God? Jesus explained, "He that believeth and is baptized shall be saved; but he that believeth not shall be damned. And these signs shall follow them that believe; In my name shall they cast out devils; they shall speak with new tongues; They shall take up serpents; and if they drink any deadly thing, it shall not hurt them; they shall lay hands on the sick, and they shall recover." (Mark 16:16-18.) It is easy to say such things are part of the Christian faith. But it is hard to do such acts. Anyone can be baptized and claim salvation. But what of the "signs that shall follow?" Are they required in order to demonstrate the existence of faith? Is Moroni's explanation right: If these things have ceased then faith has ceased and therefor none are saved? Joseph Smith thought this was exactly the case.

Therefore, he felt the obligation to teach others to develop saving faith.

Joseph was president of the church he founded for fourteen years. In that time only a few church members experienced the presence of spiritual gifts like those reported in the New Testament. Joseph acquired them for himself, but he did not seem able to help others attain them.

His final contribution in the last months of his life to the church he founded was a ceremonial ritual he called "the endowment." It was to be housed in a temple still under construction at the time he was killed. The temple rites he restored in Nauvoo, Illinois reaffirmed that God is accessible. The rites claimed, that by obedience to God's commandments, every man could receive further light and knowledge by conversing directly with the Lord through the veil. Joseph wanted God to be at the center of every Christian's faith. The temple ceremony explained that man could approach God directly and thereby avoid being "darkened in their minds by depending" on another man.

The entire Christian world shares this failure to develop sign-producing faith. When he was confronted by this failure in the people who believed he was a prophet, Joseph made the attempt to rouse others to have this faith.

The problem of weak faith was fully exposed to view by a crisis in 1831. Joseph attempted for several years to secure and convey heavenly priesthood for his followers. The quest for this priesthood began three years earlier as he was working on the *Book of Mormon* translation.

Itinerant schoolteacher, Oliver Cowdery, came to meet Joseph Smith in Harmony, Pennsylvania. He had heard rumors of gold plates while boarding with the Smith family, near Palmyra, New York. Joseph and Oliver met on April 5, 1829. The *Book of Mormon* manuscript had been underway with others transcribing, including Joseph's wife, Emma. Two days after their meeting, Cowdery became the scribe. Almost the entire *Book of Mormon* translation is in Cowdery's handwriting.

The first month Cowdery worked as Joseph's scribe, the text included accounts of baptism. This raised questions for them about receiving their own baptism. While praying in the woods, an angel claiming to be John the Baptist descended in a cloud of light and conferred on them the "Priesthood of Aaron." They were told this was the authority to baptize, but it lacked the power of laying on hands for the Holy Ghost. They were also promised by the angel that another, higher form of heavenly priesthood "would in due time be conferred upon" them. They expected something more to come later, without any specific explanation of what it was or when it would come.

They learned much more about the heavenly priesthood the next year while working on an inspired revision of the *Bible*. They began work on the inspired revision of the *Bible* in the summer of 1830. Between June and October of that year, they had replaced the first five chapters of Genesis, and by December there were seven chapters completed. These included a significant addition about Enoch and his antediluvian city called "Zion."

In December 1830, Oliver Cowdery was replaced as Joseph's scribe by a new convert named Sidney Rigdon. Rigdon had been an Alexander Campbell follower and minister. Rigdon's congregation included many who would subsequently become early converts to Mormonism.

The revisions to Genesis added significant new information about priesthood. After Christ, the two greatest priests are identified as Enoch and Melchizedek. In Joseph's revised *Bible*, much more attention is given to these two.

Enoch's priestly power caught him up to heaven, endowed him with power over the elements, and returned him to earth where he built Zion, a city of refuge. Joseph added to the biblical account the information that when Enoch was twenty-five he was ordained a priest by Adam. Then when Enoch was sixty-five, God spoke to him from heaven:

> And Enoch lived sixty-five years, and begat Methuselah, And it came to pass that Enoch journeyed in the land, among the people; and as he journeyed, the Spirit of God descended out of heaven, and abode upon him. And he heard a voice from heaven, saying: Enoch, my son, prophesy unto this people, and say unto them—Repent, for thus saith the Lord: I am angry with this people, and my fierce anger is kindled against them; for their hearts have waxed hard, and their ears are dull of hearing, and their eyes cannot see afar off[.] (Joseph Smith Translation ("JST") Genesis 6:25-27.)

God told Enoch that mankind had been denying God since the day they were created. They were murderous. They were disobedient to God's commandments. Enoch asked why he had been chosen to deliver God's message because he was slow to speak, and a lad who was not well liked. God responded by telling Enoch He would protect him, and give him the words to say.

God expanded Enoch's commission by declaring that God's Spirit would be upon Enoch and "all thy words will I justify; and the mountains shall flee before you, and the rivers shall turn from their course; and thou shalt abide in me, and I in you; therefore walk with me." (*Id.*, 6:34.) As an added power, God made Enoch a "seer" so that he would be able to see "things which were not visible to the natural eye." (*Id.*, 6:36.)

In response to his commission, Enoch preached and recorded that "all men were offended because of him." (*Id.*, 6:37.) His contemporaries declared it was a strange thing in the land because "a wild man hath come among us." (*Id.*, 6:38.) The people who heard him were afraid to hurt him because they feared God was with him. (*Id.*, 6:39.) Those who heard him hated his message, but trembled at his preaching, and could not stand in his presence. (*Id.*, 6:47.) Enoch's faith gave him power:

> So great was the faith of Enoch that he led the people of God, and their enemies came to battle against them; and he spake the word of the Lord, and the earth trembled, and the mountains fled, even according to his command; and the rivers of water were turned out of their course; and the roar of lions was heard out of the wilderness; and all nations feared greatly, so powerful was the word of Enoch, and so great was the power of the language which God had given him. (JST-Genesis 7:13.)

This great power given to Enoch allowed him to establish a city of peace. His city was called "Zion" and God descended from heaven to dwell with Enoch's people. (*Id.*, 7:17-19.) God took Enoch's city into heaven. (*Id.*, 7:21.) When the world was destroyed by flood, Enoch and his city of Zion were spared. God explained to Enoch that at the end of the world there would be another Zion established on earth.

The last days' Holy City would also be called "Zion," and would be "a New Jerusalem." Enoch's Zion would return from heaven to join with the latter-day Zion, and they would fall on each other's necks and kiss one another. (*Id.*, 7:62-63.) This would fulfill a prophecy preserved in the New

16

Testament by Jude: "Enoch also, the seventh from Adam, prophesied of these, saying Behold, the Lord cometh with ten thousands of his saints, To execute judgment upon all, and to convince all that are ungodly among them of all their ungodly deeds which they have ungodly committed, and of all their hard speeches which ungodly sinners have spoken against him." (Jude 1:14-15.) Those "ten thousands" include Enoch and his city called Zion.

This addition to Genesis made it clear that the example of Enoch needed to be repeated in the last days. God's return at the end of time required a latter-day Zion to be built. Therefore, some latter-day group must obtain the same heaven-bestowed power.

Joseph's revised *Bible* also greatly expanded information about the post-deluge patriarch Melchizedek and the priesthood he wielded. Joseph added this account to the 14th Chapter of Genesis:

> And Melchizedek lifted up his voice and blessed Abram. Now Melchizedek was a man of faith, who wrought righteousness; and when a child he feared God, and stopped the mouths of lions, and quenched the violence of fire. And thus, having been approved of God, he was ordained an high priest after the order of the covenant which God made with Enoch, It being after the order of the Son of God; And it was delivered unto men by the calling of his own voice, according to his own will, unto as many as believed on his name. For God having sworn unto Enoch and unto his seed with an oath by himself; that every one being ordained after this order and calling should have power, by faith, to break mountains, to divide the seas, to dry up waters, to turn them out of their

course; To put at defiance the armies of nations, to divide the earth, to break every band, to stand in the presence of God; to do all things according to his will, according to his command, subdue principalities and powers; and this by the will of the Son of God which was from before the foundation of the world. And men having this faith, coming up unto this order of God, were translated and taken up into heaven. And now, Melchizedek was a priest of this order; therefore he obtained peace in Salem, and was called the Prince of peace. And his people wrought righteousness, and obtained heaven, and sought for the city of Enoch which God had before taken, separating it from the earth, having reserved it unto the latter days, or the end of the world; And hath said, and sworn with an oath, that the heavens and the earth should come together; and the sons of God should be tried so as by fire. And this Melchizedek, having thus established righteousness, was called the king of heaven by his people, or, in other words, the King of peace. And he lifted up his voice, and he blessed Abram, being the high priest, and the keeper of the storehouse of God; Him whom God had appointed to receive tithes for the poor. Wherefore, Abram paid unto him tithes of all that he had, of all the riches which he possessed, which God had given him more than that which he had need. And it came to pass, that God blessed Abram, and gave unto him riches, and honor, and lands for an everlasting possession; according to the covenant which he had made, and according to the blessing wherewith Melchizedek had blessed him. (JST-Genesis 14:25-40.)

Inspired by these newly revealed accounts of priesthood, Joseph wanted to obtain it for himself and his followers. He wanted to be the one to build that New Jerusalem and establish another Zion in the last days.

Joseph's history explains his hope to receive this other, greater priesthood ordination as the angel had promised: "We now became anxious to have that promise ~~which conferred upon~~ (realized to) us, which the angel ~~had~~ that conferred upon us the Aaronick Priesthood ~~upon us~~, had given us, viz, that provided we continued faithful, ~~the~~ we should also have the Melchesidec Priesthood, which holds the authority of the laying on of hands for the gift of the Holy Ghost." (*JS Papers, Histories, Vol. 1, 1832-1844*, (Church Historian's Press: Salt Lake City, 2013), p. 326, all as in original.)

In anticipation of getting the promise fulfilled and priesthood conferred, a conference was scheduled for June 1831. Joseph promised there would be a great endowment of power given in the conference. At the conference, on June 3, 1831, a revelation to Joseph directed that twenty-three attendees were to be ordained to this heavenly priesthood. (At the time of the conference it was called "high priesthood" but later would be called "Melchizedek Priesthood.") (See "Melchizedek Priesthood" in Glossary.)

Today, the LDS church tells a different story to support their claim to have "Melchizedek Priesthood." Every LDS priesthood holder tracks his authority back to "Peter, James and John" who purportedly ordained Joseph and Oliver Cowdery on an unknown day in 1829, prior to Joseph even founding a church. The records kept contemporaneous to the events contradict the claims of the LDS church. Below are accounts written at the time of the June 1831 conference where the "high priesthood" was first given to Joseph Smith and others:

Jared Carter's journal records "Friday" (3 June) as the "memorable day when God first gave the fullness of the high priesthood to the elders of the Church of Christ." (*JS Papers, Documents Vol. 1: July 1828-June 1831*, p. 318, footnote 412, spellings as in original.)

"JS's history uses very similar language, further suggesting that *Melchizedek* was first publicly used in ordinations at the June 1831 conference: 'The authority of the Melchisedec priesthood was manifested and conferred for the first time, upon several of the elders.'" (*Id.*, p. 320, spellings and italics as in original.)

John Corrill confirms: "In John Corrill's 1839 history, he used the term *Melchizedek priesthood* instead of *high priesthood* as though the two were synonymous. He explained that 'the Malchisedec priesthood was then for the first time introduced, and conferred on several of the elders.'" (*Id.*, spellings and italics as in original.)

Parley P. Pratt confirmed the same thing. "Parley P. Pratt later explained the ordination to the high priesthood in this way: 'Several were then selected by revelation, through President Smith, and ordained to the High Priesthood after the order of the Son of God; which is after the order of Melchisedec. This was the first occasion in which this priesthood had been revealed and conferred upon the Elders in this dispensation, although the office of an Elder is the same in a certain degree, but not in the fullness. On this occasion I was ordained to this holy ordinance and calling by President Smith.' (Pratt, *Autobiography of Parley P. Pratt*, p. 72.)" (*JS Papers, Documents Vol. 1: July 1828-June 1831*, p. 318, footnote 422, spellings and cited source as in original.)

The official *History of the Church* ("DHC") published by the LDS Church states: "On the 3rd of June, the Elders from the various parts of the country where they were laboring, came in; and the conference before appointed, convened in Kirtland; and the Lord displayed His power to the most perfect satisfaction of the Saints. The man of sin was revealed, and the authority of the Melchizedek Priesthood was manifested and conferred for the first time upon several of the Elders." (*DHC*, Vol. 1, pp. 175-176.)

Joseph wanted power in the priesthood so Zion could be established in a New Jerusalem on earth. This was the priesthood Enoch used to move mountains and control rivers. As the revised version of Genesis reported, Melchizedek and "every one being ordained after this order and calling should have power, by faith, to break mountains, to divide the seas, to dry up waters, to turn them out of their course; To put at defiance the armies of nations, to divide the earth, to break every band, to stand in the presence of God; to do all things according to his will, according to his command, subdue principalities and powers; and this by the will of the Son of God which was from before the foundation of the world." This authority was necessary for Zion to be protected from destruction by the world.

In the June 1831 conference, Joseph Smith ordained five, and Lyman Wight ordained eighteen, for the total of twenty-three. For a moment they rejoiced. The heavenly priesthood returned! But the results that followed were anything but satisfactory. The authority did not "take" and the power did not come. Most of the men involved fell away and rejected Joseph shortly after their ordination. The more receptive of the men were left confused. The great blessing Joseph had waited years to receive turned into the first great crisis Joseph would confront.

"Levi Hancock, who was present at the June conference, later recalled a conversation he had in January 1832 with Lyman Wight, who ordained several individuals to the high priesthood at the June conference. Speaking about the priesthood, Hancock remarked that 'neither of us understood what it was.' 'I did not understand it,' wrote Hancock, 'and he [Wight] could give me no light.'" (*JS Papers, Documents Vol. 2: July 1831-January 1833*, p. 79.)

Not only was the ordination confusing, subsequent performance by those ordained did not mirror Melchizedek or Enoch. Of the five Joseph ordained,

-Lyman Wight was excommunicated in 1848

-Harvey Whitlock was excommunicated in 1835

-Thomas Marsh left the church in 1838, signed an affidavit against Joseph which contributed to his imprisonment in Missouri, and was excommunicated in 1839

-Parley Pratt apostatized and was excommunicated in 1842, reinstated in 1843.

Of the eighteen Lyman Wight ordained,

-John Whitmer was excommunicated in March 1838

-Sidney Rigdon was excommunicated in September 1844

-Edward Partridge died in 1840

-Ezra Thayer refused to follow the Twelve after Joseph and Hyrum were martyred

-Joseph Wakefield was excommunicated in January 1834

-Ezra Booth apostatized within months, and went on to write anti-Mormon and anti-Joseph Smith publications

-John Corrill was excommunicated in 1839

-Jacob Scott denied the faith

-Wheeler Baldwin joined the RLDS Church in 1859

Power in the Priesthood

-Martin Harris left the LDS Church, later followed James Strang, but returned to the LDS Church and was rebaptized in 1870.

None of those ordained turned rivers out of their course, divided the earth or held armies in defiance. Instead of breaking bands, they broke fellowship away from Joseph. It became apparent that ordination to this high priesthood did not confer the hoped for great endowment of power. Instead of producing power like Enoch and Melchizedek held, it produced disappointment, quickly followed by open dissent.

Ezra Booth, one of those ordained by Wight, was not content to leave quietly. He wrote a series of nine letters published in the *Ohio Star* newspaper in 1831. These were later collected by E.D. Howe and included in the 1834 anti-Mormon book *Mormonism Unvailed*. Booth was disappointed with Mormonism in general. He criticized Joseph, and pointed at the 1831 priesthood ordination as evidence of Joseph's false, grandiose pretentions. It does not appear Booth's damning letters exaggerate or misstate the events. He told his understanding of the events. He apparently thought the truth was bad enough. The Booth letters said, in relevant part:

>...Great promises are made to such as embrace it, signs and wonders are to attend them, such as healing the sick, the blind made to see, the lame to walk, &c,; and they are to receive an everlasting inheritance in "the land of Missouri," where the Savior will make his second appearance; at which place the foundation of the temple of God, and the City of Zion, have been laid, and are soon to be built. It is also to be a city of Refuge, and a safe asylum when the storms of vengeance shall pour upon the earth, and those who reject the

Book of Mormon, shall be swept off as with the besom of destruction. ... Many of them have been ordained to the High Priesthood, or the order of Melchisedec; and profess to be endowed with the same power as the ancient apostles were. But they have been hitherto unsuccessful in finding the lame, the halt, and the blind, who had faith sufficient to become the subjects of their miracles... (Ezra Booth, Letter 2, September 1831.)

...As the 4th of June last was appointed for the sessions of the conference [referring to the June 1831 conference where the ordinations occurred], it was ascertained, that that was the time specified, when the great and mighty work was to be commenced, and such was the confidence of some, that knowledge superceded their faith, and they did not hesitate to declare themselves perfectly assured that the work of miracles would commence at the ensuing conference. With such strong assurances, and with the most elevated expectations, the conference assembled at the time appointed. To give, if possible, energy to expectation, Smith, the day before the conference, professing to be filled with the spirit of prophecy, declared, that "not three days should pass away, before some should see their Savior, face to face." Soon after the session commenced, Smith arose to harangue the conference. He reminded those present of the prophecy, which he said "was given by the spirit yesterday." He wished them not to be overcome with surprise, when that event ushered in. He continued, until by long speaking, himself and some others became much excited. He then laid his hands on the head of Elder Wight, who had participated largely in the warm feeling of his leader, and ordained him to the High Priesthood. He was set apart for the service of the Indians, and was ordained to the gift of tongues, healing the sick, casting out devils, and discerning spirits; and in like manner he ordained several others; and then called upon Wight to take the floor. Wight arose, and presented a pale countenance, a fierce look, with arms extended, and his hands cramped back, the whole system agitated, and a very unpleasant object to look upon. He exhibited himself as an instance of the great power of God, and called upon those around him "if you want to see a sign, look at me." He then stepped upon a bench, and declared with a loud voice, he saw the Savior: and thereby, for the time being, rescued Smith's prophecy from merited contempt. —It, however, procured Wight the authority to ordain the rest. So said the spirit, and so said Smith. The spirit in Smith selected those to be ordained, and the spirit in Wight ordained them. But the spirit in Wight proved an erring dictator; so much so, that some of the candidates felt the weight of hands thrice, before the work was rightly done. Another Elder, who had been ordained to the same office as Wight, at the bidding of Smith, stepped upon the floor. Then ensued a scene, of which you can form no adequate conception; and which, I would forbear relating, did not the truth require it. The Elder moved upon the floor, his legs inclining to a bend; one shoulder elevated above the other, upon which the head seemed disposed to recline, his arms partly extended; his hands partly clenched; his mouth partly open, and contracted in the shape of an italic O; his eyes assumed a wild ferocious cast, and his whole appearance presented a frightful object to the view of the beholder. – "Speak, Brother Harvey" said Smith. But Harvey intimated by signs, that his power of articulation was in a state of suspense, and that he was unable to speak. Some conjectured that Harvey was possessed of the devil, but Smith said, "the Lord binds in order to set at liberty." After different opinions had been given, and there had been much confusion, Smith learnt by the spirit, that Harvey was under a diabolical influence, and that Satan had bound him; and he commanded the unclean spirit to come out of him. It now became clearly manifest, that "the man of sin was revealed," for the express purpose that the elders should become acquainted with the devices of Satan; and after that they would possess knowledge sufficient to manage him. This, Smith declared to be a miracle, and his success in this case, encouraged him to work other and different miracles. Taking the hand of one of the Elders in his own, a hand which by accident had been rendered defective, he said, "Brother Murdock, I command you in the name of Jesus Christ to straighten your hand;" in the mean while endeavoring to accomplish the work by using his own hand to open the hand of the other. The effort proved unsuccessful; but he again articulated the same commandment, in a more authoritative and louder tone of voice; and while uttering with his tongue, his hands were at work; but after all the exertion of his power, both natural and supernatural, the deficient hand returned to its former position, where it still remains. But ill success in this case, did not discourage him from undertaking another. One of the Elders who was decrepit in one of his legs, was set upon the floor, and commanded, in the name of Jesus Christ to walk. He walked a step or two, his faith failed, and he was again compelled to have recourse to his former assistant, and he has had occasion to use it ever since. A dead body. Which had been retained above ground two or three days, under the expectation that the dead would be raised, was insensible to the voice of those who commanded it to awake into life, and is destined to sleep in the grave till the last trump shall sound, and the power of God easily accomplishes the work, which frustrated the attempts, and bid defiance to the puny efforts of the Mormonite.** That an attempt was made to raise the child, is denied, of course, as every other attempt has been, after the entire failure was obvious to all. The parents of the deceased child, however, state, that they were prevented from procuring medical aid for the child, by the representations of the elders, that there was no danger -- that it would certainly be restored.

27

The father had no other idea but that the child was to be raised; neither did his faith fail him till preparations were made for its interment. He then awoke from his dream of delusion, and dissolved his connection with the impostors. Under these discouraging circumstances, the horizon of Mormonism gathered darkness, and a storm seemed to hang impending over the church. The gloom of disappointed expectation, overspread the countenances of many, while they labored to investigate the cause of this failure. To add, if possible, to their mortification, a larger assembly collected on the Sabbath, in order to hear preaching. In the midst of the meeting the congregation was dismissed by Rigdon, and the people sent to their homes. He was directed to do this, he said, by the spirit. But it was generally believed, that he was directed solely by fear; and that he had mistaken the spirit of cowardice, for the spirit of the Lord. Several of the Elders said they "felt the spirit to preach" to the congregation: and Rigdon felt the spirit to send the people home: such was the unity which then prevailed among them. You will doubtless say, can it be possible that the minds of men, and men who possess the appearance of honesty, can be so strangely infatuated, as still to adhere to a system, after it had occasioned so much agitation, and so much disappointment. One reason which can be assigned for this, is, the adherents are generally inclined to consider the system so perfect, as to admit of no suspicion; and the confusion and disappointment, are attributed to some other cause. Another, and principal reason is, delusion always effects the mind with a species of delirium, and this delirium arises in a degree proportionate to the magnitude of the delusion. These men, upon other subjects, will converse like other men; but when their favorite system is brought into view, its inconsistencies and contradictions are resolved into inexplicable mystery; and this will not only apply to the delusions now under consideration, but in my view, to every delusion, from the highest to the lowest; and it matters not whether it carries the stamp of popularity or its opposite. (Ezra Booth, Letter 3, September 1831.)

These harsh but candid words were printed in the local newspaper immediately before a second conference in October 1831. Joseph again conferred the high priesthood on a second group during that conference. It is noteworthy, that despite his failure in June, Joseph tried again in October.

In addition to the discouraged participants, there were others who reflected on the ordinations for years before concluding Joseph made a mistake. David Whitmer (one of the Three Witnesses to the *Book of Mormon*) was not present when the first ordinations took place. He heard of them, and read the account written by his brother John, the church historian. David Whitmer remained faithful for seven more years. However, later he would claim that he never believed these ordinations were proper, and would dissent and reject Joseph's leadership altogether. Eventually he published a stinging criticism of the ordinations performed in June 1831 as improper and unscriptural. He retold early Mormon history in his pamphlet, *Address to All Believers in Christ*, published in

1887. It included these reflections regarding the June 1831 conference:

> This matter of priesthood, since the days of Sydney Rigdon, has been the great hobby and stumbling block of the Latter Day Saints. Priesthood means authority; and authority is the word we should use. I do not think the word priesthood is mentioned in the New Covenant of the Book of Mormon. Authority is the word we used for the first two years in the church—until Sydney Rigdon's days in Ohio. This matter of the two orders of priesthood in the Church of Christ, and lineal priesthood of the old law being in the church, all originated in the mind of Sydney Rigdon. ...In Kirtland, Ohio, in June, 1831, at a conference of the church, the first High Priests were ordained into the church. Brother Joseph ordained Lyman Wight, John Murdock, Harvey Whitlock, Hyrum Smith, Reynolds Cahoon and others to the office of a High Priest. When they were ordained, right there at the time, the devil caught and bound Harvey Whitlock so he could not speak, his face being twisted into demon-like shape. Also John Murdock and others were caught by the devil in a similar manner. How brethren, do you not see that the displeasure of the Lord was upon their proceedings in ordaining High Priests? Of course it was. These facts are recorded in the History of the Church—written by my brother, John Whitmer, who was the regularly appointed church historian. I was not at that conference, being then in Hiram, which is near Kirtland,

Ohio. I also have the testimony of Harvey Whitlock whom the devil caught and bound; also John Whitmer, who was present, and others who were present at the time, so I know it is true. (*An Address to All Believers in Christ*, Chapter 9: High Priests.)

Joseph's followers may have been confused and discouraged by the priesthood ordination, but he was not. They did not share his vision, but that did not discourage Joseph. He proceeded with confidence and conviction to help others see that something great could be gained from heavenly priesthood. He never showed any sign of doubt about his own experience with God and angels. He described his certainty: "I had seen a vision; I knew it, and I knew that God knew it, and I could not deny it, neither dared I do it; at least I knew that by so doing I would offend God, and come under condemnation." (JS-H 1:25.) Because Joseph was certain God appeared to and spoke with him, there was nothing in the priesthood failure to cause him doubt. Despite the mess created by Ezra Booth's nine letters, Joseph proceeded confidently to address his followers' lack of faith.

At the next round of ordinations in October 1831, Joseph tried to address the problem directly. This time, Joseph instructed, admonished and encouraged, while Rigdon warned about God's rejection of them if they failed to faithfully measure up. The minutes of the conference report that Joseph Smith told the new priests, "It is the privilege of every Elder to speak of the things of God &c, And could we all come together with one heart and one mind in perfect faith the vail [sic] might as well be rent to day as next week or any other time and if we will but cleanse ourselves and covenant before God, to serve him, it is our privilege to have an assurance [sic] that God will protect us at all times." (*JS Papers, Documents, Vol. 2: July 1831-January 1833*, p. 81.) He continued, "the order of the High priesthood is that they have power given them to seal up the Saints unto eternal life. And said it was the privilege of every Elder present to be ordained to the Highpriesthood [sic]." (*Id.* at p. 82.)

Sidney Rigdon was far less encouraging. He warned the newly ordained, "it was the privilege of those Elders present to be ordained to the High Priesthood, telling them that if they then should doubt God would withdraw his Spirit from them." (*Id.* p. 83.) Thereafter Joseph interviewed the candidates. He concluded, "he had a testimony that each had one talent and if after being ordained they should hide it God would take it from them." (*Id.* p. 86.)

As the conference concluded, Rigdon was apparently unimpressed with some of the new priests. His closing comments included this frank assessment, "the Lord was not well pleased with some of them because of their indifference to be ordained to that office, exhortation to faith and obedience setting forth the power of that office." (*Id.*) These conference minutes reveal the low expectations of both Joseph and Sidney Rigdon. Low expectations were justified. No mountains moved, no rivers turned out of their course, and Zion did not appear.

Still Joseph was not shaken in his belief that God would allow mankind to receive the same miraculous priesthood the ancients held. The power, visions, control over elements, and outpouring of gifts would be given again. He likewise believed God had authorized it to be conferred. But nothing positive happened. Ordinations had been most noteworthy in what they did NOT accomplish. Those ordained did not even remain faithful. The dilemma was how to fix the failure. Joseph did not view the meager results as evidence of his or God's inability, but man's. Joseph often explained that a man was saved no faster than he gains knowledge. (See, e.g., *TPJS*, p. 217; D&C 130: 18-19.) Therefore, the failure could be cured if only those ordained learned enough to become adept priests.

In this first, great crisis, Joseph Smith's response reveals more about him than all that happened before in his life. He composed a series of lectures designed to teach others how to have faith. These lectures were delivered first orally, and later published. When printed in 1835 as part of a volume of new scripture titled *Doctrine and Covenants*, Joseph edited the lectures and vouched for them as true doctrine. The lectures were the first portion of the book, and constituted the "Doctrine" of the volume. The *Lectures* were part of the Mormon scripture from 1835 until they were later dropped. The various Mormon churches discarded them, until only the LDS church retained them as scripture. In 1921, a committee of LDS church leaders thought the lectures had errors. Mormonism's founder prepared the lectures to encourage faith. Later Mormon leaders discarded them because they did not have any faith in their reliability.

In 2010, Boyd K. Packer, the President of the Twelve Apostles for the LDS Church, lamented in general conference that their church lacked priesthood power. As he put it, "We have done very well at distributing the *authority* of the priesthood. We have priesthood authority planted nearly everywhere. We have quorums of elders and high priests worldwide. But distributing the *authority* of the priesthood has raced, I think, ahead of distributing the *power* of the priesthood. The priesthood does not have the strength that it should have and will not have until the *power* of the priesthood is firmly fixed in the families as it should be." (Boyd K. Packer, *The Power of the Priesthood*, April 2010 LDS General Conference, emphasis in original.) Joseph Smith provided the cure for the lack of priesthood power in *Lectures on Faith*. But the LDS Church discarded *Lectures* only to find they are now just like the confused and powerless 1831 priests.

The problem Joseph encountered with the believers in 1831 remains the problem for all Christians: How is faith in God developed? The solution Joseph advanced to solve the problem, *Lectures on Faith*, has been discarded by every church claiming him as a founder. It is not likely these churches can ever hope to achieve power in their priesthood if they reject Joseph Smith's thoughtful response to the problem. But there is no reason other Christians cannot benefit from the instructions.

While considering Joseph's response, bear in mind he already claimed to have seen God, been visited by angels, and received ordination with authority to baptize others. He was not hoping to advance his personal spiritual life. This was his effort solely to help others achieve similar spiritual advancement. Joseph Smith's written response to the first great crisis is set out in the next chapter. This material was once considered scripture. He wrote it intending for all believers to use the information to get closer to God.

LECTURES ON FAITH
BY JOSEPH SMITH
...THE CARE OF ALL THE CHURCHES

Lecture First:

1. Faith being the first principle in revealed religion, and the foundation of all righteousness, necessarily claims the first place in a course of lectures which are designed to unfold to the understanding the doctrine of Jesus Christ.

2. In presenting the subject of faith, we shall observe the following order:

3. First, Faith itself—what it is:

4. Secondly, The object on which it rests; and

5. Thirdly, The effects which flow from it.

6. Agreeably to this order we have first to show what faith is.

7. The author of the epistle to the Hebrews, in the eleventh chapter of that epistle, and first verse, gives the following definition of the word faith:

8. Now faith is the substance [assurance] of things hoped for, the evidence of things not seen.

9. From this we learn, that faith is the assurance which men have of the existence of things which they have not seen; and the principle of action in all intelligent beings.

10. If men were duly to consider themselves, and turn their thoughts and reflections to the operations of their own minds, they would readily discover that it is faith, and faith only, which is the moving cause of all action, in them; that without it, both mind and body would be in a state of

inactivity, and all their exertions would cease, both physical and mental.

11. Were this class to go back and reflect upon the history of their lives, from the period of their first recollection, and ask themselves, what principle excited them to action, or what gave them energy and activity, in all their lawful avocations, callings and pursuits, what would be the answer? Would it not be that it was the assurance which we had of the existence of things which we had not seen, as yet?—Was it not the hope which you had, in consequence of your belief in the existence of unseen things, which stimulated you to action and exertion, in order to obtain them? Are you not dependent on your faith, or belief, for the acquisition of all knowledge, wisdom and intelligence? Would you exert yourselves to obtain wisdom and intelligence, unless you did believe that you could obtain them? Would you have ever sown if you had not believed that you would reap? Would you have ever planted if you had not believed that you would gather? Would you have ever asked unless you had believed that you would receive? Would you have ever sought unless you had believed that you would have found? Or would you have ever knocked unless you had believed that it would have been opened unto you? In a word, is there any thing that you would have done, either physical or mental, if you had not previously believed? Are not all your exertions, of every kind, dependent on your faith? Or may we not ask, what have you, or what do you possess, which you have not obtained by reason of your faith? Your food, your raiment, your lodgings, are they not all by reason of your faith? Reflect, and ask yourselves, if these things are not so. Turn your thoughts on your own minds, and see if faith is not the moving cause of all action in yourselves; and if the moving cause in you, is it not in all other intelligent beings?

36

12. And as faith is the moving cause of all action in temporal concerns, so it is in spiritual; for the Savior has said, and that truly, that he that believeth and is baptized, shall be saved. (Mark 16:16)

13. As we receive by faith, all temporal blessings that we do receive, so we, in like manner, receive by faith all spiritual blessings, that we do receive. But faith is not only the principle of action, but of power, also, in all intelligent beings, whether in heaven, or on earth. Thus says the author of the epistle to the Hebrews, 11:3:

14. "Through faith we understand that the worlds were framed by the word of God: so that things which are seen were not made of things which do appear."

15. By this we understand that the principle of power, which existed in the bosom of God, by which the worlds were framed, was faith; and that it is by reason of this principle of power, existing in the Deity, that all created things exist—so that all things in heaven, on earth, or under the earth, exist by reason of faith, as it existed in HIM.

16. Had it not been for the principle of faith the worlds would never have been framed, neither would man have been formed of the dust—it is the principle by which Jehovah works, and through which he exercises power over all temporal, as well as eternal things. Take this principle or attribute, (for it is an attribute) from the Deity and he would cease to exist.

17 Who cannot see, that if God framed the worlds by faith, that it is by faith that he exercises power over them, and that faith is the principle of power? And that if the principle of power, it must be so in man as well as in the Deity? This is the testimony of all the sacred writers, and the lesson which they have been endeavoring to teach to man.

18. The Savior says, (Matthew 17:19-20), in explaining the reason why the disciples could not cast out the devil, that it

was because of their unbelief: "For verily, I say unto you," said he, "if ye have faith as a grain of mustard-seed, ye shall say unto this mountain, 'Remove hence to yonder place,' and it shall remove; and nothing shall be impossible unto you."

19. Moroni, while abridging and compiling the record of his fathers, has given us the following account of faith as the principle of power: He says, in Ether 12:13, that it was the faith of Alma and Amulek which caused the walls of the prison to be rent, as recorded in Alma 14:23-29; it was the faith of Nephi and Lehi which caused a change to be wrought upon the hearts of the Lamanites, when they were immersed with the Holy Spirit, and with fire, as seen in Helaman 5:37-50; and that it was by faith that the mountain Zerin was removed, when the brother of Jared spake in the name of the Lord. See also Ether 12:30.

20. In addition to this we are told in Hebrews, 11:32-35, that Gideon, Barak, Samson, Jephthah, David, Samuel, and the prophets, through faith subdued kingdoms, wrought righteousness, obtained promises, stopped the mouths of lions, quenched the violence of fire, escaped the edge of the sword, out of weakness were made strong, waxed valiant in fight, turned to flight the armies of the aliens; and that women received their dead raised to life again, etc.

21. Also, Joshua, in the sight of all Israel, bade the sun and moon to stand still, and it was done. (Joshua 10:12)

22. We here understand, that the sacred writers say, that all these things were done by faith—It was by faith that the worlds were framed—God spake, chaos heard, and worlds came into order, by reason of the faith there was in HIM. So with man also—he spake by faith in the name of God, and the sun stood still, the moon obeyed, mountains removed, prisons fell, lions' mouths were closed, the human heart lost its enmity, fire its violence, armies their power, the sword its

terror, and death its dominion; and all this by reason of the faith which was in them.

23. Had it not been for the faith which was in man, they might have spoken to the sun, the moon, the mountains, prisons, lions, the human heart, fire, armies, the sword, or to death in vain!

24. Faith, then, is the first great governing principle which has power, dominion, and authority over all things: by it they exist, by it they are upheld, by it they are changed, or by it they remain, agreeably to the will of God. Without it, there is no power, and without power there could be no creation, nor existence!

Lecture Second:

1. Having shown in our previous lecture "faith itself— what it is," we shall proceed to show secondly the object on which it rests.

2. We here observe that God is the only supreme governor, and independent being, in whom all fulness and perfection dwells; who is omnipotent, omnipresent, and omniscient; without beginning of days or end of life; and that in him every good gift, and every good principle dwells; and that he is the Father of lights: In him the principle of faith dwells independently; and he is the object in whom the faith of all other rational and accountable beings centers, for life and salvation.

3. In order to present this part of the subject in a clear and conspicuous point of light, it is necessary to go back and show the evidences which mankind have had, and the foundation on which these evidences are, or were based, since the creation, to believe in the existence of a God.

4. We do not mean those evidences which are manifested by the works of creation, which we daily behold with our natural eyes: we are sensible, that after a revelation of Jesus Christ, the works of creation, throughout their vast forms and

varieties, clearly exhibit his eternal power and Godhead. Romans 1:20: For the invisible things of him from the creation of the world are clearly seen, being understood by the things that are made: even his eternal power and Godhead. But we mean those evidences by which the first thoughts were suggested to the minds of men that there was a God who created all things.

5. We shall now proceed to examine the situation of man at his first creation. Moses, the historian, has given us the following account of him in the first chapter of the book of Genesis, beginning with the 20th verse, and closing with the 30th. We copy from the new translation:

6. And the Lord God said unto the Only Begotten, who was with him from the beginning, Let us make man in our image, after our likeness: and it was done.

7. And the Lord God said, Let them have dominion over the fish of the sea, and over the fowl of the air, and over the cattle, and over all the earth, and over every creeping thing that creeps upon the earth.

8. So God created man in his own image, in the image of the Only Begotten created he him; male and female created he them. And God blessed them, and God said unto them, Be fruitful, and multiply, and replenish the earth, and subdue it: and have dominion over the fish of the sea, and over the fowl of the air, and over every living thing that moves upon the earth.

9. And the Lord God said unto man, Behold, I have given you every herb bearing seed, which is upon the face of all the earth, and every tree in the which is the fruit of a tree yielding seed; to you it shall be for meat.

10. Again, Genesis 2:15-17,19-20: And the Lord God took the man, and put him into the garden of Eden, to dress it and to keep it. And the Lord God commanded the man, saying, Of every tree of the garden you may freely eat: but of

the tree of the knowledge of good and evil you shall not eat of it, neither shall you touch it; nevertheless, you may choose for yourself, for it is given unto you; but remember that I forbid it: for in the day that you eat thereof you shall surely die.

11. And out of the ground the Lord God formed every beast of the field, and every fowl of the air, and commanded that they should be brought unto Adam, to see what he would call them. And whatever Adam called every living creature, that was the name thereof. And Adam gave names to all cattle, and to the fowl of the air, and to every beast of the field.

12. From the foregoing we learn man's situation at his first creation; the knowledge with which he was endowed, and the high and exalted station in which he was placed—lord, or governor of all things on earth, and at the same time enjoying communion and intercourse with his Maker, without a veil to separate between. We shall next proceed to examine the account given of his fall, and of his being driven out of the garden of Eden, and from the presence of the Lord.

13. Moses proceeds: And they [Adam and Eve] heard the voice of the Lord God as they were walking in the garden in the cool of the day, and Adam and his wife hid themselves from the presence of the Lord God among the trees of the garden. And the Lord God called unto Adam, and said unto him, Where are you going? And he said, I heard your voice in the garden, and I was afraid, because I beheld that I was naked, and I hid myself.

14. And the Lord God said unto Adam, Who told you that you were naked? Have you eaten of the tree whereof I told you that you should not eat? If so, you should surely die? And the man said, The woman whom you gave me, and commanded that she should remain with me, gave me of the fruit of the tree, and I did eat.

41

15. And the Lord God said unto the woman, What is this which you have done? And the woman said, The serpent beguiled me, and I did eat.

16. And again, the Lord said unto the woman, I will greatly multiply your sorrow, and your conception: in sorrow you shall bring forth children; and your desire shall be to your husband, and he shall rule over you.

17. And the Lord God said unto Adam, because you have hearkened unto the voice of your wife, and have eaten of the fruit of the tree of which I commanded you, saying, You shall not eat of it! cursed shall be the ground for your sake: in sorrow you shall eat of it all the days of your life. Thorns also, and thistles shall it bring forth to you: and you shall eat the herb of the field. By the sweat of your face shall you eat bread, until you shall return unto the ground—for you shall surely die—for out of it you were taken; for dust you were, and unto dust you shall return. This was immediately followed by the fulfillment of what we previously said: Man was driven, or sent out of Eden.

18. Two important items are shown from the former quotations: First, After man was created, he was not left without intelligence, or understanding, to wander in darkness, and spend an existence in ignorance and doubt—on the great and important point which effected his happiness—as to the real fact by whom he was created, or unto whom he was amenable for his conduct. God conversed with him face to face: in his presence he was permitted to stand, and from his own mouth he was permitted to receive instruction—he heard his voice, walked before him, and gazed upon his glory—while intelligence burst upon his understanding, and enabled him to give names to the vast assemblage of his Maker's works.

19. Secondly, we have seen, that though man did transgress, his transgression did not deprive him of the

previous knowledge with which he was endowed, relative to the existence and glory of his Creator; for no sooner did he hear his voice, than he sought to hide himself from his presence.

20. Having shown, then, in the first instance, that God began to converse with man, immediately after he "breathed into his nostrils the breath of life," and that he did not cease to manifest himself to him, even after his fall, we shall next proceed to show, that, though he was cast out from the garden of Eden, his knowledge of the existence of God was not lost, neither did God cease to manifest his will unto him.

21. We next proceed to present the account of the direct revelation which man received, after he was cast out of Eden, and further copy from the new translation:

22. After Adam had been driven out of the garden, he began to till the earth, and to have dominion over all the beasts of the field, and to eat his bread by the sweat of his brow, as I, the Lord had commanded him: and he called upon the name of the Lord, and so did Eve his wife also. And they heard the voice of the Lord from the way toward the garden of Eden, speaking unto them; and they saw him not, for they were shut out from his presence: but he gave unto them commandments that they should worship the Lord their God, and should offer the firstlings of their flocks for an offering unto the Lord. And Adam was obedient unto the commandment.

23. And after many days an angel of the Lord appeared unto Adam, saying, why do you offer sacrifices unto the Lord? And Adam said unto him, I know not; but the Lord commanded me to offer sacrifices.

24. And the angel said unto him, This thing is a similitude of the sacrifice of the Only Begotten of the Father, who is full of grace and truth. And you shall do all that you do in the name of the Son: and you shall repent and call upon God in

his name forever. In that day the Holy Spirit fell upon Adam, and bore record of the Father and the Son.

25. This last quotation, or summary, shows this important fact, that though our first parents were driven out of the garden of Eden, and were even separated from the presence of God, by a vail, they still retained a knowledge of his existence, and that sufficiently to move them to call upon him. And further, that no sooner was the plan of redemption revealed to man, and he began to call upon God, than the Holy Spirit was given, bearing record of the Father and Son.

26. Moses also gives us an account, in the 4th of Genesis, of the transgression of Cain, and the righteousness of Abel, and of the revelations of God to them. He says, "In process of time Cain brought of the fruit of the ground, an offering unto the Lord—And Abel also brought of the firstlings of his flock, and of the fat thereof. And the Lord had respect unto Abel, and to his offering: but unto Cain and to his offering he had not respect. Now satan knew this, and it pleased him. And Cain was very angry, and his countenance fell. And the Lord said unto Cain, 'Why are you angry? Why is your countenance fallen? If you do well, will you not be accepted? And if you do not well, sin lies at the door, and satan desires to have you; and except you shall hearken unto my commandments, I will deliver you up: and it shall be unto you according to his desire.'

27. "And Cain went into the field and talked with his brother Abel. And while they were in the field, Cain rose up against his brother Abel, and slew him. And Cain gloried in what he had done, saying, 'I am free; surely the flocks of my brother will now fall into my hands.'

28. "But the Lord said unto Cain, 'Where is Abel, your brother?' And he said, 'I know not: am I my brother's keeper?' And the Lord said, 'What have you done? the voice of your brother's blood cries unto me from the ground. And

now, you shall be cursed from the earth which has opened her mouth to receive your brother's blood, from your hand. When you till the ground, she shall not henceforth yield unto you her strength. A fugitive and a vagabond also, you shall be in the earth.'

29. "And Cain said unto the Lord, 'Satan tempted me because of my brother's flocks. And I was also angry: for his offering was accepted, and mine was not: My punishment is greater than I can bear. Behold, you have driven me out this day from the face of men, and from your face shall I be hid also; and I shall be a fugitive and a vagabond in the earth; and it shall come to pass, every one that finds me will slay me, because of my oath; for these things are not hid from the Lord.' And the Lord said unto him, 'Therefore, whoever slays Cain, vengeance shall be taken on him seven fold.' And the Lord set a mark upon Cain, lest any finding him should kill him."

30. The object of the foregoing quotations is to show to this class the way by which mankind were first made acquainted with the existence of a God: that it was by a manifestation of God to man, and that God continued, after man's transgression to manifest himself to him and his posterity: and notwithstanding they were separated from his immediate presence, that they could not see his face, they continued to hear his voice.

31. Adam thus being made acquainted with God, communicated the knowledge which he had unto his posterity; and it was through this means that the thought was first suggested to their minds that there was a God. Which laid the foundation for the exercise of their faith, through which they could obtain a knowledge of his character and also of his glory.

32. Not only was there a manifestation made unto Adam of the existence of a God, but Moses informs us, as before

quoted, that God condescended to talk with Cain after his great transgression, in slaying his brother, and that Cain knew that it was the Lord that was talking with him: so that when he was driven out from the presence of his brethren, he carried with him the knowledge of the existence of a God: and through this means, doubtless his posterity became acquainted with the fact that such a being existed.

33. From this we can see that the whole human family, in the early age of their existence, in all their different branches, had this knowledge disseminated among them; so that the existence of God became an object of faith, in the early age of the world. And the evidences which these men had of the existence of a God, was the testimony of their fathers in the first instance.

34. The reason why we have been thus particular on this part of our subject, is, that this class may see by what means it was that God became an object of faith among men after the fall; and what it was that stirred up the faith of multitudes to feel after him; to search after a knowledge of his character, perfections and attributes, until they became extensively acquainted with him; and not only commune with him, and behold his glory, but be partakers of his power, and stand in his presence.

35. Let this class mark particularly that the testimony which these men had of the existence of a God, was the testimony of man; for previous to the time that any of Adam's posterity had obtained a manifestation of God to themselves, Adam their common father had testified unto them of the existence of God, and of his eternal power and Godhead.

36. For instance, Abel, before he received the assurance from heaven that his offerings were acceptable unto God, had received the important information of his father, that such a being did exist, who had created, and who did uphold all

things. Neither can there be a doubt existing on the mind of any person, that Adam was the first who did communicate the knowledge of the existence of a God, to his posterity; and that the whole faith of the world, from that time down to the present, is in a certain degree, dependent on the knowledge first communicated to them by their common progenitor; and it has been handed down to the day and generation in which we live, as we shall show from the face of the sacred records.

37. First, Adam was 130 years old when Seth was born (Genesis 5:3). And the days of Adam, after he had begotten Seth, were 800 years; making him 930 years old when he died (Genesis 5:4-5). Seth was 105 when Enos was born (v.6); Enos was 90 when Cainan was born (v.9); Cainan was 70 when Mahalaleel was born (v.12); Mahalaleel was 65 when Jared was born (v.15); Jared was 162 when Enoch was born (v.18); Enoch was 65 when Methuselah was born (v.21); Methuselah was 187 when Lamech was born (v.25); Lamech was 182 when Noah was born (v.28).

38. From this account it appears that Lamech, the 9th from Adam, and the father of Noah, was 56 years old when Adam died; Methuselah, 243; Enoch, 308; Jared 470; Mahalaleel, 535; Cainan, 605; Enos, 695; and Seth, 800.

39. So that Lamech, the father of Noah; Methuselah, Enoch, Jared, Mahalaleel, Cainan, Enos, Seth, and Adam, were all living at the same time, and beyond all controversy, were all preachers of righteousness.

40. Moses further informs us, that Seth lived, after he begat Enos, 807 years; making him 912 years old at his death (Genesis 5:7-8). And Enos lived, after he begat Cainan, 815 years: making him 905 years old when he died (vv.10-11). And Cainan lived, after he begat Mahalaleel, 840 years: making him 910 years old at his death (vv.13-14). And Mahalaleel lived, after he begat Jared, 830 years: making him 895 years old when he died (vv.16-17). And Jared lived, after he begat

Enoch, 800 years: making him 962 years old at his death (vv.19-20). And Enoch walked with God, after he bagat Methuselah, 300 years: making him 365 years old when he was translated (vv.22,23). And Methuselah lived, after he begat Lamech, 782 years: making him 969 years old when he died (vv.26-27). Lamech lived, after he begat Noah, 595 years: making him 777 years old when he died (vv.30-31).

41. Agreeably to this account, Adam died in the 930th year of the world, Enoch was translated in the 987th, Seth died in the 1042nd, Enos in the 1140th, Cainan in the 1235th, Mahalaleel in the 1290th, Jared in the 1422nd, Lamech in the 1651st, and Methuselah in the 1656th, it being the same year in which the flood came.

42. So that Noah was 84 years old when Enos died, 176 when Cainan died, 234 when Mahalaleel died, 366 when Jared died, 595 when Lamech died, and 600 when Methuselah died.

43. We can see from this that Enos, Cainan, Mahalaleel, Jared, Methuselah, Lamach, and Noah all lived on the earth at the same time, And that Enos, Cainan, Mahalaleel, Jared, Methuselah, and Lamech, were all acquainted with both Adam and Noah.

44. From the foregoing it is easily to be seen, not only how the knowledge of God came into the world, but upon what principle it was preserved: that from the time it was first communicated, it was retained in the minds of righteous men, who taught, not only their own posterity, but the world; so that there was no need of a new revelation to man, after Adam's creation, to Noah, to give them the first idea, or notion of the existence of a God: and not only of a God, but of the true and living God.

45. Having traced the chronology of the world from Adam to Noah, we will now trace it from Noah to Abraham. Noah was 502 years old when Shem was born: 98 years afterward the flood came, being the 600th year of Noah's age.

And Moses informs us that Noah lived after the flood, 350 years: making him 950 years old when he died. (Genesis 9:28-29.)

46. Shem was 100 years old when Arphaxed was born. (Genesis 11:10.) Arphaxed was 35 when Salah was born (11:12); Salah was 30 when Eber was born (11:14); Eber was 34 when Peleg was born: in whose days the earth was divided (11:16); Peleg was 30 when Reu was born (11:18); Reu was 32 when Serug was born (11:20); Serug was 30 when Nahor was born (11:22); Nahor was 29 when Terah was born (11:24); Terah was 70 when Haran and Abraham were born (11:26).

47. There is some difficulty in the account given by Moses, of Abraham's birth. Some have supposed, that Abraham was not born until Terah was 130 years old. This conclusion is drawn from a variety of scriptures, which are not to our purpose at present to quote. Neither is it a matter of any consequence to us, whether Abraham was born when Terah was 70 years old, or 130. But in order that there may no doubt exist upon any mind, in relation to the object lying immediately before us, in presenting the present chronology, we will date the birth of Abraham at the latest period: that is, when Terah was 130 years old. It appears from this account, that from the flood to the birth of Abraham was 352 years.

48. Moses informs us that Shem lived, after, he begat Arphaxed, 500 years (11:11); This added to 100 years, which was his age when Arphaxed was born, makes him 600 years old when he died. Arphaxed lived, after he begat Salah, 403 years (11:13); This added to 35 years, which was his age when Salah was born, makes him 438 years old when he died. Salah lived, after he begat Eber, 403 years (11:15); this added to 30 years, which was his age when Eber was born, makes him 433 years old when he died. Eber lived, after he begat Peleg, 430 years (11:17); this added to 34 years, which was his age when Peleg was born, makes him 464 years old. Peleg lived, after he

begat Reu, 209 years (11:19); this added to 30 years, which was his age when Reu was born, makes him 239 years old when he died. Reu lived, after he begat Serug, 207 years (11:21); this added to 32 years, which was his age when Serug was born, makes him 239 years old when he died. Serug lived, after he begat Nahor, 200 years (11:23); this added to 30 years, which was his age when Nahor was born, makes him 230 years old when he died. Nahor lived, after he begat Terah, 119 years (11:25); this added to 29 years, which was his age when Terah was born, makes him 148 years old when he died. Terah was 130 years old when Abraham was born, and is supposed to have lived 75 years after his birth: making him 205 years old when he died.

49. Agreeably to this last account, Peleg died in the 1996th year of the world. Nahor in the 1997th, and Noah in the 2006th. So that Peleg, in whose days the earth was divided, and Nahor, the grand-father of Abraham, both died before Noah: the former being 239 years old, and the latter 148. And who cannot but see, that they must have had a long and intimate acquaintance with Noah?

50. Reu died in the, 2026th year of the world, Serug in 2049th, Terah in the 2083rd, Arphaxed in the 2096th, Salah in the 2126th, Shem in the 2158th, Abraham in the 2183rd, and Eber in the 2187th: which was 4 years after Abraham's death. And Eber was the fourth from Noah.

51. Nahor, Abraham's brother, was 58 years old when Noah died, Terah 128, Serug 187, Reu 219, Eber 283, Salah 313, Arphaxed 344, and Shem 448.

52. It appears from this account, that Nahor, brother of Abraham, Terah, Nahor, Serug, Reu, Peleg, Eber, Salah, Arphaxed, Shem, and Noah, all lived on the earth at the same time. And that Abraham was 18 years old when Reu died, 41 when Serug and his brother Nahor died, 75 when Terah died, 88 when Arphaxed died, 118 when Salah died, 150 when

Shem died, and that Eber lived 4 years after Abraham's death. And that Shem, Arphaxed, Salah, Eber, Reu, Serug, Terah, and Nahor, the brother of Abraham, and Abraham, lived at the same time. And that Nahor, brother of Abraham, Terah, Serug, Reu, Eber, Salah, Arphaxed, and Shem, were all acquainted with both Noah and Abraham.

53. We have now traced the chronology of the world, agreeably to the account given in our present Bible, from Adam to Abraham, and have clearly determined, beyond the power of controversy, that there was no difficulty in preserving the knowledge of God in the world, from the creation of Adam, and the manifestation made to his immediate descendants, as set forth in the former part of this lecture, so that the students, in this class need not have any dubiety resting on their minds, on this subject; for they can easily see, that it is impossible for it to be otherwise; but that the knowledge of the existence of a God, must have continued from father to son, as a matter of tradition, at least. For we cannot suppose, that a knowledge of this important fact, could have existed in the mind of any of the before mentioned individuals, without their having made it known to their posterity.

54. We have now shown how it was that the first thought ever existed in the mind of any individual, that there was such a being as a God, who had created and did uphold all things: that it was by reason of the manifestation which he first made to our father Adam, when he stood in his presence, and conversed with him face to face, at the time of his creation.

55. Let us here observe, that after any portion of the human family are made acquainted with the important fact that there is a God who has created and does uphold all things, the extent of their knowledge, respecting his character and glory, will depend upon their diligence and faithfulness in seeking after him, until like Enoch the brother of Jared, and

Moses, they shall obtain faith in God, and power with him to behold him face to face.

56. We have now clearly set forth how it is, and how it was, that God became an object of faith for rational beings; and also, upon what foundation the testimony was based, which excited the enquiry and diligent search of the ancient saints, to seek after and obtain a knowledge of the glory of God: and we have seen that it was human testimony, and human testimony only, that excited this enquiry, in the first instance in their minds—it was the credence they gave to the testimony of their fathers—this testimony having aroused their minds to enquire after the knowledge of God, the enquiry frequently terminated, indeed, always terminated, when rightly pursued, in the most glorious discoveries, and eternal certainty.

Lecture Third:

1. In the second lecture it was shown, how it was that the knowledge of the existence of God, came into the world, and by what means the first thoughts were suggested to the minds of men, that such a being did actually exist: and that it was by reason of the knowledge of his existence, that there was a foundation laid for the exercise of faith in him, as the only being in whom faith could center for life and salvation. For faith could not center in a Being of whose existence we had no idea; because the idea of his existence in the first instance is essential to the exercise of faith in him. Romans 10:14: "How then shall they call on him in whom they have not believed? And how shall they believe in him of whom they have not heard? And how shall they hear without a preacher?" (or one sent to tell them?) "So then faith comes by hearing the word of God."

2. Let us here observe, that three things are necessary, in order that any rational and intelligent being may exercise faith in God unto life and salvation.

3. First, the idea that he actually exists.

4. Secondly, a correct idea of his character, perfections and attributes.

5. Thirdly, an actual knowledge that the course of life which he is pursuing, is according to his will.—For without an acquaintance with these three important facts, the faith of every rational being must be imperfect and unproductive; but with this understanding, it can become perfect and fruitful, abounding in righteousness unto the praise and glory of God the Father, and the Lord Jesus Christ.

6. Having previously been made acquainted with the way the idea of his existence came into the world, as well as the fact of his existence, we shall proceed to examine his character, perfections and attributes, in order that this class may see, not only the just grounds which they have for the exercise of faith in him, for life and salvation, but the reasons that all the world, also, as far as the idea of his existence extends, may have to exercise faith in him the Father of all living.

7. As we have been indebted to a revelation which God made of himself to his creatures in the first instance, for the idea of his existence, so in like manner we are indebted to the revelations which he has given to us, for a correct understanding of his character, perfections and attributes; because without the revelations which he has given to us, no man by searching could find out God (Job 11:7-9). 1 Cor. 2:9-11: "But as it is written, eye has not seen, nor ear heard, neither have entered into the heart of man, the things which God has prepared for them that love him; but God has revealed them unto us by his Spirit: for the Spirit searches all things, yea, the deep things of God. For what man knows the things of a man, save the spirit of man which is in him? Even so, the things of God no man knows but by the Spirit of God."

8. Having said so much, we proceed to examine the character which the revelations have given of God.

9. Moses gives us the following account in Exodus, 34:6: "And the Lord passed by before him, and proclaimed, The Lord God, the Lord God, merciful and gracious, long suffering, and abundant in goodness and truth." Psalms 103:6-8: "The Lord executes righteousness and judgment for all that are oppressed. He made known his ways unto Moses, his acts unto the children of Israel. The Lord is merciful and gracious, slow to anger and plenteous in mercy:" Psalms 103:17-18: "But the mercy of the Lord is from everlasting to everlasting upon them that fear him, and his righteousness unto children's children, to such as keep his covenant, and to those that remember his commandments to do them." Psalms 90:2: "Before the mountains were brought forth, or ever you had formed the earth and the world, even from everlasting to everlasting, you are God." Hebrews 1:10-12: "And you, Lord, in the beginning have laid the foundation of the earth; and the heavens are the works of your hands: they shall perish, but you shall remain; and they shall wax old as a garment; and as a vesture shall you fold them up, and they shall be changed: but you are the same, and your years shall not fail." James 1:17: "Every good gift, and every perfect gift, is from above, and comes down from the Father of lights; with whom is no variableness, neither shadow of turning." Malachi 3:6: "For I am the Lord, I change not; therefore ye sons of Jacob are not consumed."

10. *Book of Commandments*, chapter 3, verse 2: "For God does not walk in crooked paths, neither does he turn to the right hand or the left, or vary from that which he has said, therefore his paths are strait, and his course is one eternal round:" *Book of Commandments*, chapter 35:1: "Listen to the voice of the Lord your God, even Alpha and Omega, the

beginning and the end, whose course is one eternal round, the same yesterday to-day and forever."

11. Numbers 23:19: "God is not a man, that he should lie; neither the son of man that he should repent." 1 John 4:8: "He that loves not, knows not God; for God is love." Acts 10:34: "Then Peter opened his mouth and said, Of a truth I perceive that God is no respecter of persons, but in every nation he that fears God and works righteousness is accepted with him."

12. From the foregoing testimonies, we learn the following things respecting the character of God.

13. First, that he was God before the world was created, and the same God that he was, after it was created.

14. Secondly, that he is merciful, and gracious, slow to anger, abundant in goodness, and that he was so from everlasting, and will be to everlasting.

15. Thirdly, that he changes not, neither is there variableness with him; but that he is the same from everlasting to everlasting, being the same yesterday to-day and forever; and that his course is one eternal round, without variation.

16. Fourthly, that he is a God of truth and cannot lie.

17. Fifthly, that he is no respecter of persons; but in every nation he that fears God and works righteousness is accepted of him.

18.   Sixthly, that he is love.

19. An acquaintance with these attributes in the divine character, is essentially necessary, in order that the faith of any rational being can center in him for life and salvation. For if he did not, in the first instance, believe him to be God, that is, the creator and upholder of all things, he could not center his faith in him for life and salvation, for fear there should be a greater than he, who would thwart all his plans, and he, like the gods of the heathen, would be unable to fulfill his

promises; but seeing he is God over all, from everlasting to everlasting, the creator and upholder of all things, no such fear can exist in the minds of those who put their trust in him, so that in this respect their faith can be without wavering.

20. But, secondly; unless he was merciful and gracious, slow to anger, long suffering, and full of goodness, such is the weakness of human nature, and so great the frailties and imperfections of men, that unless they believed that these excellencies existed in the divine character, the faith necessary to salvation could not exist; for doubt would take the place of faith, and those who know their weakness and liability to sin, would be in constant doubt of salvation, if it were not for the idea which they have of the excellency of the character of God, that he is slow to anger, and long suffering, and of a forgiving disposition, and does forgive iniquity, transgression and sin. An idea of these facts does away with doubt, and makes faith exceedingly strong.

21. But it is equally as necessary that men should have the idea that he is a God who changes not, in order to have faith in him, as it is to have the idea that he is gracious and long suffering. For without the idea of unchangeableness in the character if the Deity, doubt would take the place of faith. But with the idea that he changes not, faith lays hold upon the excellencies in his character with unshaken confidence, believing he is the same yesterday, to-day and forever, and that his course is one eternal round.

22. And again, the idea that he is a God of truth and cannot lie, is equally as necessary to the exercise of faith in him, as the idea of his unchangeableness. For without the idea that he was a God of truth and could not lie, the confidence necessary to be placed in his word in order to the exercise of faith in him, could not exist. But having the idea that he is not man that he can lie, it gives power to the minds of men to exercise faith in him.

23. But it is also necessary that men should have an idea that he is no respecter of persons; for with the idea of all the other excellencies in his character, and this one wanting, men could not exercise faith in him, because if he were a respecter of persons, they could not tell what their privileges were, nor how far they were authorized to exercise faith in him, or whether they were authorized to do it at all, but all must be confusion; but no sooner are the minds of men made acquainted with the truth on this point, that he is no respecter of persons, than they see that they have authority by faith to lay hold on eternal life the richest boon of heaven, because God is no respecter of persons, and that every man in every nation has an equal privilege.

24. And lastly, but not less important to the exercise of faith in God, is the idea that he is love; for with all the other excellencies in his character, without this one to influence them, they could not have such powerful dominion over the minds of men; but when the idea is planted in the mind that he is love, who cannot see the just ground that men of every nation, kindred and tongue, have to exercise faith in God so as to obtain eternal life?

25. From the above description of the character of the Deity which is given him in the revelations, to men, there is a sure foundation for the exercise of faith in him among every people, nation and kindred, from age to age, and from generation to generation.

26. Let us here observe that the foregoing is the character which is given of God in his revelations to the Former Day Saints, and it is also the character which is given of him in his revelations to the Latter Day Saints, so that the saints of former days, and those of latter days, are both alike in this respect; the Latter Day Saints having as good grounds to exercise faith in God, as the Former Day Saints had; because the same character is given of him to both.

Lecture Fourth:

1. Having shown in the third lecture, that correct ideas of the character of God are necessary in order to the exercise of faith in him unto life and salvation, and that without correct ideas of his character, the minds of men could not have sufficient power with God to the exercise of faith necessary to the enjoyment of eternal life, and that correct ideas of his character lay a foundation as far as his character is concerned, for the exercise of faith, so as to enjoy the fulness of the blessing of the gospel of Jesus Christ, even that of eternal glory; we shall now proceed to show the connection there is between correct ideas of the attributes of God, and the exercise of faith in him unto eternal life.

2. Let us here observe, that the real design which the God of heaven had in view in making the human family acquainted with his attributes, was, that they through the ideas of the existence of his attributes, might be enabled to exercise faith in him, and through the exercise of faith in him, might obtain eternal life. For without the idea of the existence of the attributes which belong to God, the minds of men could not have power to exercise faith on him so as to lay hold upon eternal life. The God of heaven understanding most perfectly the constitution of human nature, and the weakness of man, knew what was necessary to be revealed, and what ideas must be planted in their minds in order that they might be enabled to exercise faith in him unto eternal life.

3. Having said so much we shall proceed to examine the attributes of God, as set forth in his revelations to the human family, and to show how necessary correct ideas of his attributes are, to enable men to exercise faith in him. For without these ideas being planted in the minds of men, it would be out of the power of any person or persons to exercise faith in God so as to obtain eternal life. So that the divine communications made to man in the first instance,

58

were designed to establish in their minds the ideas necessary to enable them to exercise faith in God, and through this means to be partakers of his glory.

4. We have, in the revelations which he has given to the human family, the following account of his attributes.

5. First, knowledge. Acts 15:18: "Known unto God are all his works from the beginning of the world." Isaiah 46:9-10: "Remember the former things of old; for I am God and there is none else; I am God, and there is none like me, declaring the end from the beginning, and from ancient time the things that are not yet done, saying, My counsel shall stand, and I will do all my pleasure."

6. Secondly, faith, or power. Hebrews 11:3: "Through faith we understand that the worlds were framed by the word of God." Genesis 1:1: "In the beginning God created the heaven and the earth." Isaiah 14:24,27: "The Lord of hosts has sworn, saying, Surely as I have thought so shall it come to pass; and as I have purposed, so shall it stand. For the Lord of hosts has purposed, and who shall disannul it? and his hand is stretched out, and who shall turn it back?"

7. Thirdly, justice. Psalms 89:14: "Justice and judgment are the habitation of thy throne." Isaiah 45:21: "Tell ye, and bring them near; yea, let them take council together: who has declared this from the ancient time? Have not I the Lord? and there is no God else beside me; a just God and a Savior." Zephaniah 5:5: "The just Lord is in the midst thereof." Zechariah 9:9: "Rejoice greatly, O daughter of Zion; shout, O daughter of Jerusalem: behold, thy King comes unto thee: he is just, and having salvation."

8. Fourthly, judgment. Psalms 89:14: "Justice and judgment are the habitation of thy throne." Deuteronomy 32:4: "He is the Rock, his work is perfect; for all his ways are judgment: a God of truth, and without iniquity: just and right is he." Psalms 9:7: "But the Lord shall endure forever: he has

prepared his throne for judgment." Psalms 9:16: "The Lord is
known by the judgment which he executes."

9. Fifthly, mercy. Psalms 89:15: "Mercy and truth shall go
before his face." Exodus 34:6: "And the Lord passed by
before him, and proclaimed, The Lord, the Lord God,
merciful and gracious." Nehemiah 9:17: "But thou art a God
ready to pardon, gracious and merciful."

10. And Sixthly, truth. Psalms 89:14: "Mercy and truth
shall go before thy face." Exodus 34:6: "Long suffering and
abundant in goodness and truth." Deuteronomy 32:4: "He is
the Rock, his work is perfect; for all his ways are judgment. A
God of truth and without iniquity: just and right is he."
Psalms 31:5: "Into thy hand I commit my spirit: thou hast
redeemed me, O Lord God of truth."

11. By a little reflection it will be seen, that the idea of the
existence of these attributes in the Deity, is necessary to
enable any rational being to exercise faith in him. For without
the idea of the existence of these attributes in the Deity, men
could not exercise faith in him for life and salvation; seeing
that without the knowledge of all things, God would not be
able to save any portion of his creatures; for it is by reason of
the knowledge which he has of all things, from the beginning
to the end, that enables him to give that understanding to his
creatures, by which they are made partakers of eternal life;
and if it were not for the idea existing in the minds of men,
that God had all knowledge, it would be impossible for them
to exercise faith in him.

12. And it is not less necessary that men should have the
idea of the existence of the attribute power in the Deity. For,
unless God had power over all things, and was able, by his
power, to control all things, and thereby deliver his creatures
who put their trust in him, from the power of all beings that
might seek their destruction, whether in heaven, on earth, or
in hell, men could not be saved; but with the idea of the

existence of this attribute, planted in the mind, men feel as though they had nothing to fear, who put their trust in God, believing that he has power to save all who come to him, to the very uttermost.

13. It is also necessary, in order to the exercise of faith in God, unto life and salvation, that men should have the idea of the existence of the attribute justice, in him. For without the idea of the existence of the attribute Justice, in the Deity, men could not have confidence sufficiently to place themselves under his guidance and direction; for they would be filled with fear and doubt, lest the Judge of all the earth would not do right; and thus fear, or doubt, existing in the mind, would preclude the possibility of the exercise of faith in him for life and salvation. But, when the idea of the existence of the attribute justice, in the Deity, is fairly planted in the mind, it leaves no room for doubt to get into the heart, and the mind is enabled to cast itself upon the Almighty without fear and without doubt, and with most unshaken confidence, believing that the Judge of all the earth will do right.

14. It is also of equal importance that men should have the idea of the existence of the attribute judgment, in God, in order that they may exercise faith in him for life and salvation; for without the idea of the existence of this attribute in the Deity, it would be impossible for men to exercise faith in him for life and salvation, seeing that it is through the exercise of this attribute that the faithful in Christ Jesus are delivered out of the hands of those who seek their destruction; for if God were not to come out in swift judgment against the workers of iniquity and the powers of darkness, his saints could not be saved; for it is by judgment that the Lord delivers his saints out of the hands of all their enemies, and those who reject the gospel of our Lord Jesus Christ. But no sooner is the idea of the existence of this attribute, planted in the minds of men, than it gives power to the minds for the exercise of faith and

confidence in God, and they are enabled, by faith, to lay hold on the promises which are set before them, and wade through all the tribulations and afflictions to which they are subjected by reason of the persecution from those who know not God, and obey not the gospel of our Lord Jesus Christ: believing, that in due time the Lord will come out in swift judgment against their enemies, and they shall be cut off from before him, and that in his own due time he will bear them off conquerers and more than conquerers in all things.

15. And again, it is equally important that men should have the idea of the existence of the attribute mercy, in the Deity, in order to exercise faith in him for life and salvation. For, without the idea of the existence of this attribute in the Deity, the spirits of the saints would faint in the midst of the tribulations, afflictions and persecutions which they have to endure for righteousness' sake; but when the idea of the existence of this attribute is once established in the mind it gives life and energy to the spirits of the saints: believing that the mercy of God will be poured out upon them in the midst of their afflictions, and that he will be compassionate for them in their sufferings; and that the mercy of God will lay hold of them and secure them in the arms of his love, so that they will receive a full reward for all their sufferings.

16. And lastly, but not less important to the exercise of faith in God, is the idea of the existence of the attribute truth, in him. For, without the idea of the existence of this attribute the mind of man could have nothing upon which it could rest with certainty: all would be confusion and doubt; but with the idea of the existence of this attribute in the Deity, in the mind, all the teachings, instructions, promises and blessings become realities, and the mind is enabled to lay hold of them with certainty and confidence: believing that these things, and all that the Lord has said, shall be fulfilled in their time; and that all the cursings, denunciations and judgments,

pronounced upon the heads of the unrighteous will also be executed in the due time of the Lord: and by reason of the truth and veracity of him, the mind beholds its deliverance and salvation as being certain.

17. Let the mind once reflect sincerely and candidly upon the ideas of the existence of the before mentioned attributes in the Deity, and it will be seen, that as far as his attributes are concerned, there is a sure foundation laid for the exercise of faith in him for life and salvation. For in as much as God possesses the attribute knowledge he can make all things known to his saints necessary for their salvation; and as he possesses the attribute power he is able thereby to deliver them from the power of all enemies; and seeing also, that justice is an attribute of the Deity, he will deal with them upon the principles of righteousness and equity, and a just reward will be granted unto them for all their afflictions and sufferings for the truth's sake. And as judgment is an attribute of the Deity also, his saints can have the most unshaken confidence, that they will, in due time, obtain a perfect deliverance out of the hands of all their enemies, and a complete victory over all those who have sought their hurt and destruction. And as mercy is also an attribute of the Deity, his saints can have confidence that it will be exercised toward them; and through the exercise of that attribute toward them, comfort and consolation will be administered unto them abundantly, amid all their afflictions and tribulations. And lastly, realizing that truth is an attribute of the Deity, the mind is led to rejoice amid all its trials and temptations, in hope of that glory which is to be brought at the revelation of Jesus Christ, and in view of that crown which is to be placed upon the heads of the saints in the day when the Lord shall distribute rewards unto them, and in prospect of that eternal weight of glory which the Lord has

promised to bestow upon them when he shall bring them into the midst of his throne to dwell in his presence eternally.

18. In view, then, of the existence of these attributes, the faith of the saints can become exceedingly strong: abounding in righteousness unto the praise and glory of God, and can exert its mighty influence in searching after wisdom and understanding, until it has obtained a knowledge of all things that pertain to life and salvation.

19. Such, then, is the foundation, which is laid, through the revelation of the attributes of God, for the exercise of faith in him for life and salvation; and seeing that these are attributes of the Deity, they are unchangeable—being the same yesterday to day and forever—which gives to the minds of the Latter Day Saints the same power and authority to exercise faith in God, which the Former Day Saints had: so that all the saints, in this respect have been, are and will be alike, until the end of time; for God never changes, therefore his attributes and character remain forever the same. And as it is through the revelation of these that a foundation is laid for the exercise of faith in God unto life and salvation, the foundation, therefore, for the exercise of faith, was, is and ever will be the same; so that all men have had, and will have an equal privilege.

Lecture Fifth:

1. In our former lectures we treated of the being, character, perfections and attributes of God. What we mean by perfections, is, the perfections which belong to all the attributes of his nature. We shall, in this lecture speak of the Godhead: we mean the Father, Son and Holy Spirit.

2. There are two personages who constitute the great, matchless, governing and supreme power over all things—by whom all things were created and made, that are created and made, whether visible or invisible: whether in heaven, on earth, or in the earth, under the earth, or throughout the

immensity of space—They are the Father and the Son: The Father being a personage of spirit, glory and power: possessing all perfection and fulness: The Son, who was in the bosom of the Father, a personage of tabernacle, made, or fashioned like unto man, or being in the form and likeness of man, or, rather, man was formed after his likeness, and in his image;—he is also the express image and likeness of the personage of the Father: possessing all the fulness of the Father, or, the same fulness with the Father; being begotten of him, and was ordained from before the foundation of the world to be a propitiation for the sins of all those who should believe on his name, and is called the Son because of the flesh—and descended in suffering below that which man can suffer, or, in other words, suffered greater sufferings, and was exposed to more powerful contradictions than any man can be. But notwithstanding all this, he kept the law of God, and remained without sin: Showing thereby that it is in the power of man to keep the law and remain also without sin. And also, that by him a righteous judgment might come upon all flesh, and that all who walk not in the law of God, may justly be condemned by the law, and have no excuse for their sins. And he being the only begotten of the Father, full of grace and truth, and having overcome, received a fulness of the glory of the Father—possessing the same mind with the Father, which mind is the Holy Spirit, that bears record of the Father and the Son, and these three are one, or in other words, these three constitute the great, matchless, governing and supreme power over all things: by whom all things were created and made, that were created and made: and these three constitute the Godhead, and are one: The Father and the Son possessing the same mind, the same wisdom, glory, power and fulness: Filling all in all—the Son being filled with the fulness of the Mind, glory and power, or, in other words, the Spirit, glory and power of the Father—possessing all knowledge and glory, and the same kingdom: sitting at the right hand of power, in the express image and likeness of the Father—a Mediator for man—being filled with the fulness of the Mind of the Father, or, in other words, the Spirit of the Father: which Spirit is shed forth upon all who believe on his name and keep his commandments: and all those who keep his commandments shall grow up from grace to grace, and become heirs of the heavenly kingdom, and joint heirs with Jesus Christ; possessing the same mind, being transformed into the same image or likeness, even the express image of him who fills all in all: being filled with the fulness of his glory, and become one in him, even as the Father, Son and Holy Spirit are one.

3. From the foregoing account of the Godhead, which is given in his revelations, the Saints have a sure foundation laid for the exercise of faith unto life and salvation, through the atonement and mediation of Jesus Christ, by whose blood they have a forgiveness of sins, and also, a sure reward laid up for them in heaven, even that of partaking of the fulness of the Father and the Son, through the Spirit. As the Son partakes of the fulness of the Father through the Spirit, so the saints are, by the same Spirit, to be partakers of the same fulness, to enjoy the same glory; for as the Father and the Son are one, so in like manner the saints are to be one in them, through the love of the Father, the mediation of Jesus Christ, and the gift of the Holy Spirit; they are to be heirs of God and joint heirs with Jesus Christ.

Lecture Sixth:

1. Having treated, in the preceding lectures, of the ideas of the character, perfections and attributes of God, we next proceed to treat of the knowledge which persons must have, that the course of life which they pursue is according to the will of God, in order that they may be enabled to exercise faith in him unto life and salvation.

66

Lectures on Faith

2. This knowledge supplies an important place in revealed religion; for it was by reason of it that the ancients were enabled to endure as seeing him who is invisible. An actual knowledge to any person that the course of life which he pursues is according to the will of God, is essentially necessary to enable him to have that confidence in God, without which no person can obtain eternal life. It was this that enabled the ancient saints to endure all their afflictions and persecutions, and to take joyfully the spoiling of their goods, knowing, (not believing merely), that they had a more enduring substance (Hebrews 10:34).

3. Having the assurance that they were pursuing a course which was agreeable to the will of God, they were enabled to take, not only the spoiling of their goods, and the wasting of their substance, joyfully, but also to suffer death in its most horrid forms; knowing, (not merely believing), that when this earthly house of their tabernacle was dissolved, they had a building of God, a house not made with hands, eternal in the heavens (2 Corinthians 5:1).

4. Such was and always will be the situation of the saints of God, that unless they have an actual knowledge that the course that they are pursuing is according to the will of God, they will grow weary in their minds and faint; for such has been and always will be the opposition in the hearts of unbelievers and those that know not God, against the pure and unadulterated religion of heaven, (the only thing which ensures eternal life), that they will persecute, to the uttermost, all that worship God according to his revelations, receive the truth in the love of it, and submit themselves to be guided and directed by his will, and drive them to such extremities that nothing short of an actual knowledge of their being the favorites of heaven, and of their having embraced that order of things which God has established for the redemption of man, will enable them to exercise that confidence in him

necessary for them to overcome the world, and obtain that crown of glory which is laid up for them that fear God.

5. For a man to lay down his all, his character and reputation, his honor and applause, his good name among men, his houses, his lands, his brothers and sisters, his wife and children, and even his own life also, counting all things but filth and dross for the excellency of the knowledge of Jesus Christ, requires more than mere belief, or supposition that he is doing the will of God, but actual knowledge: realizing, that when these sufferings are ended he will enter into eternal rest; and be a partaker of the glory of God.

6. For unless a person does know that he is walking according to the will of God, it would be offering an insult to the dignity of the Creator, were he to say that he would be a partaker of his glory when he should be done with the things of this life. But when he has this knowledge, and most assuredly knows that he is doing the will of God, his confidence can be equally strong that he will be a partaker of the glory of God.

7. Let us here observe, that a religion that does not require the sacrifice of all things, never has power sufficient to produce the faith necessary unto life and salvation; for from the first existence of man, the faith necessary unto the enjoyment of life and salvation never could be obtained without the sacrifice of all earthly things: it was through this sacrifice, and this only, that God has ordained that men should enjoy eternal life; and it is through the medium of the sacrifice of all earthly things, that men do actually know that they are doing the things that are well pleasing in the sight of God. When a man has offered in sacrifice all that he has, for the truth's sake, not even withholding his life, and believing before God that he has been called to make this sacrifice, because he seeks to do his will, he does know most assuredly, that God does and will accept his sacrifice and offering, and

68

that he has not nor will not seek his face in vain. Under these circumstances, then, he can obtain the faith necessary for him to lay hold on eternal life.

8. It is in vain for persons to fancy to themselves that they are heirs with those, or can be heirs with them, who have offered their all in sacrifice, and by this means obtained faith in God and favor with him so as to obtain eternal life, unless they in like manner offer unto him the same sacrifice, and through that offering obtain the knowledge that they are accepted of him.

9. It was in offering sacrifices that Abel, the first martyr, obtained knowledge that he was accepted of God. And from the days of righteous Abel to the present time, the knowledge that men have that they are accepted in the sight of God, is obtained by offering sacrifice: and in the last days, before the Lord comes, he is to gather together his saints who have made a covenant with him by sacrifice. Psalms 50:3-5: "Our God shall come, and shall not keep silence: a fire shall devour before him, and it shall be very tempestuous round about him. He shall call to the heavens from above, and to the earth, that he may judge his people. Gather my saints together unto me; those that have made a covenant unto me by sacrifice."

10. Those, then, who make the sacrifice will have the testimony that their course is pleasing in the sight of God, and those who have this testimony will have faith to lay hold on eternal life, and will be enabled, through faith, to endure unto the end, and receive the crown that is laid up for them that love the appearing of our Lord Jesus Christ. But those who do not make the sacrifice cannot enjoy this faith, because men are dependent upon this sacrifice in order to obtain this faith; therefore, they cannot lay hold upon eternal life, because the revelations of God do not guarantee unto them

the authority so to do; and without this guarantee faith could not exist.

11. All the saints of whom we have account in all the revelations of God which are extant, obtained the knowledge which they had of their acceptance in his sight, through the sacrifice which they offered unto him: and through the knowledge thus obtained, their faith became sufficiently strong to lay hold upon the promise of eternal life, and to endure as seeing him who is invisible; and were enabled, through faith, to combat the powers of darkness, contend against the wiles of the adversary, overcome the world, and obtain the end of their faith, even the salvation of their souls.

12. But those who have not made this sacrifice to God, do not know that the course which they pursue is well pleasing in his sight; for whatever may be their belief or their opinion, it is a matter of doubt and uncertainty in their mind; and where doubt and uncertainty is, there faith is not, nor can it be. For doubt and faith do not exist in the same person at the same time. So that persons whose minds are under doubts and fears cannot have unshaken confidence, and where unshaken confidence is not, there faith is weak, and where faith is weak, the persons will not be able to contend against all the opposition, tribulations and afflictions which they will have to encounter in order to be heirs of God, and joint heirs with Christ Jesus; and they will grow weary in their minds, and the adversary will have power over them and destroy them.

Lecture Seventh:

1. In the preceding lectures, we treated of what faith was, and of the object on which it rested; agreeably to our plan we now proceed to speak of its effects.

2. As we have seen in our former lectures, that faith was the principle of action and of power in all intelligent beings, both in heaven and on earth, it will not be expected that we

will, in a lecture of this description attempt to unfold all its effects; neither is it necessary to our purpose so to do; for it would embrace all things in heaven and on earth, and encompass all the creations of God, with all their endless varieties: for no world has yet been framed that was not framed by faith; neither has there been an intelligent being on any of God's creations who did not get there by reason of faith, as it existed in himself or in some other being; nor has there been a change or a revolution in any of the creations of God but it has been effected by faith: neither will there be a change or a revolution unless it is effected in the same way, in any of the vast creations of the Almighty; for it is by faith that the Deity works.

3. Let us here offer some explanation in relation to faith that our meaning may be clearly comprehended: We ask, then, what are we to understand by a man's working by faith? We answer: We understand that when a man works by faith he works by mental exertion instead of physical force: it is by words instead of exerting his physical powers, with which every being works when he works by faith—God said, Let there be light, and there was light—Joshua spake and the great lights which God had created stood still—Elijah commanded and the heavens were stayed for the space of three years and six months, so that it did not rain: He again commanded, and the heavens gave forth rain,–all this was done by faith; and the Savior says, If you have faith as a grain of mustard seed, say to this mountain, remove, and it will remove; or say to that sycamore tree, Be ye plucked up and planted in the midst of the sea, and it shall obey you. Faith, then, works by words; and with these its mightiest works have been, and will be performed.

4. It surely will not be required of us to prove, that this is the principle upon which all eternity has acted and will act; for every reflecting mind must know, that it is by reason of this

power that all the hosts of heaven perform their works of wonder, majesty and glory: Angels move from place to place by virtue of this power—it is by reason of it that they are enabled to descend from heaven to earth; and were it not for the power of faith they never could be ministering spirits to them who should be heirs of salvation, neither could they act as heavenly messengers; for they would be destitute of the power necessary to enable them to do the will of God.

5. It is only necessary for us to say, that the whole visible creation, as it now exists, is the effect of faith—It was faith by which it was framed, and it is by the power of faith that it continues in its organized form, and by which the planets move round their orbits and sparkle forth their glory: So, then, faith is truly the first principle in the science of theology, and when understood, leads the mind back to the beginning and carries it forward to the end; or in other words, from eternity to eternity.

6. As faith, then, is the principle by which the heavenly hosts perform their works, and by which they enjoy all their felicity, we might expect to find it set forth in a revelation from God as the principle upon which his creatures, here below, must act, in order, to obtain the felicities enjoyed by the saints in the eternal world, and that when God would undertake to raise up men for the enjoyment of himself, he would teach them the necessity of living by faith, and the impossibility there was of their enjoying the blessedness of eternity without it, seeing that all the blessings of eternity are the effects of faith.

7. Therefore, it is said, and appropriately too, that "without faith it is impossible to please God." If it should be asked: Why is it impossible to please God without faith? The answer would be: Because without faith it is impossible for men to be saved; and as God desires the salvation of men, he must, of course, desire that they should have faith; and he

could not be pleased unless they had, or else he could be pleased with their destruction.

8. From this we learn that the many exhortations which have been given by inspired men to those who had received the word of the Lord, to have faith in him, were not mere common-place matters, but were for the best of all reasons, and that was, because, without it there was no salvation, neither in this world nor in that which is to come. When men begin to live by faith they begin to draw near to God; and when faith is perfected they are like him; and because he is saved they are saved also; for they will be in the same situation he is in, because they have come to him; and when he appears they shall be like him, for they will see him as he is.

9. As all the visible creation is an effect of faith, so is salvation, also. (We mean salvation in its most extensive latitude of interpretation, whether it is temporal or spiritual.) In order to have this subject clearly set before the mind, let us ask what situation must a person be in, in order to be saved? or what is the difference between a saved man and one who is not saved? We answer from what we have before seen of the heavenly worlds, they must be persons who can work by faith, and who are able, by faith to be ministering spirits to them who shall be heirs of salvation. And they must have faith to enable them to act in the presence of the Lord, otherwise they cannot be saved. And what constitutes the real difference between a saved person and one not saved, is the difference in the degree of their faith: one's faith has become perfect enough to lay hold upon eternal life, and the other's has not. But to be a little more particular, let us ask, where shall we find a prototype into whose likeness we may be assimilated, in order that we may be made partakers of life and salvation? or in other words, where shall we find a saved being? for if we can find a saved being, we may ascertain

without much difficulty what all others must be in order to be saved; for whatever constitutes the salvation of one, will constitute the salvation of every creature which will be saved; and if we find one saved being in all existence, we may see what all others must be, or else not be saved. We ask, then, where is the prototype? or where is the saved being? We conclude as to the answer of this question, there will be no dispute among those who believe the Bible, that it is Christ: all will agree in this that he is the prototype or standard of salvation, or in other words, that he is a saved being. And if we should continue our interrogation, and ask how it is that he is saved? the answer would be, because he is a just and holy being; and if he were any thing different from what he is he would not be saved; for his salvation depends on his being precisely what he is and nothing else; for if it were possible for him to change in the least degree, so sure he would fail of salvation and lose all his dominion, power, authority and glory, which constitutes salvation; for salvation consists in the glory, authority, majesty, power and dominion which Jehovah possesses, and in nothing else; and no being can possess it but himself or one like him: Thus says John, in his first epistle, 3:2 and 3: "Behold, now we are the sons of God, and it doth not appear what we shall be; but we know, that when he shall appear we shall be like him; for we shall see him as he is. And any man that has this hope in him purifies himself, even as he is pure."—Why purify himself as he is pure? Because if they do not they cannot be like him.

10. The Lord said unto Moses, Leviticus, 19:2: "Speak unto all the congregation of the children of Israel, and say unto them, Ye shall be holy: for I the Lord your God am holy." And Peter says, first epistle, 1:15-16: "But as he who has called you is holy, so be ye holy in all manner of conversation; because it is written, Be ye holy; for I am holy." And the Savior says, Matthew 15:48: "Be ye perfect, even as

74

your Father who is in heaven is perfect." If any should ask why all these sayings? the answer is to be found from what is before quoted from John's epistle, that when he (the Lord) shall appear, the saints will be like him: and if they are not holy, as he is holy, and perfect as he is perfect, they cannot be like him; for no being can enjoy his glory without possessing his perfections and holiness, no more than they could reign in his kingdom without his power.

11. This clearly sets forth the propriety of the Savior's saying, recorded in John's testimony, 4:12: "Verily, verily I say unto you, he that believeth on me, the works that I do shall he do also; and greater works than these, because I go unto the Father."—This taken in connection with some of the sayings in the Savior's prayer, recorded in the 17th chapter, gives great clearness to his expressions: He says, in the 20-24: "Neither pray I for these alone; but for them also who shall believe on me through their words; that they all may be one, as thou, Father art in me, and I in thee, that they also may be one in us: that the world may believe that thou hast sent me. And the glory which thou gavest me, I have given them, that they may be one, even as we are one; I in them, and thou in me, that they may be made perfect in one; and that the world may know that thou hast sent me, and hast loved them as thou hast loved me, Father, I will that they also whom thou hast given me be with me where I am: that they may behold my glory which thou hast given me; for thou lovest me before the foundation of the world."

12. All these sayings put together, give as clear an account of the state of the glorified saints as language could give— The works that Jesus had done they were to do, and greater works than those which he done among them should they do, and that because he went to the Father. He does not say that they should do these works in time; but they should do greater works because he went to the Father. He says, in the

24th verse: "Father, I will that they also whom thou hast given me, be with me where I am; that they may behold my glory." These sayings, taken in connection, make it very plain, that the greater works, which those that believed on his name, were to do, were to be done in eternity, where he was going, and where they should behold his glory. He had said, in another part of his prayer, that he desired of his Father, that those who believed on him should be one in him, as he, and the Father were one in each other: Neither pray I for these (the apostles) alone, but for them also who shall believe on me through their words; that they all may be one: that is, they who believe on him through the apostles' words, as well as the apostles themselves: that they all may be one, as thou, Father, art in me and I in thee: that they also may be one in us.

13. What language can be plainer than this? The Savior surely intended to be understood by his disciples: and he so spake that they might understand him; for he declares to his Father, in language not to be easily mistaken, that he wanted his disciples, even all of them, to be as himself and the Father: for as he and the Father were one, so they might be one with them. And what is said in the 22nd verse is calculated to more firmly establish this belief, if it needs any thing to establish it. He says, "And the glory which thou gavest me, I have given them, that they may be one, even as we are one." As much as to say, that unless they have the glory which the Father had given him, they could not be one with them: For he says he had given them the glory that the Father had given him, that they might be one; or in other words, to make them one.

14. This fills up the measure of information on this subject, and shows most clearly, that the Savior wished his disciples to understand, that they were to be partakers with him in all things: not even his glory excepted.

15. It is scarcely necessary here to observe what we have previously noticed: That the glory which the Father and the Son have, is because they are just and holy beings; and that if they were lacking in one attribute or perfection which they have, the glory which they have, never could be enjoyed by them; for it requires them to be precisely what they are in order to enjoy it: and if the Savior gives this glory to any others, he must do it in the very way set forth in his prayer to his Father: by making them one with him, as he and the Father are one.—In so doing he would give them the glory which the Father has given him; and when his disciples are made one with the Father and the Son, as the Father and the Son are one, who cannot see the propriety of the Savior's saying, "The works which I do, shall they do; and greater works than these shall they do, because I go to the Father?"

16. These teachings of the Savior must clearly show unto us the nature of salvation; and what he proposed unto the human family when he proposed to save them—That he proposed to make them like unto himself; and he was like the Father, the great prototype of all saved beings: And for any portion of the human family to be assimilated into their likeness is to be saved; and to be unlike them is to be destroyed: and on this hinge turns the door of salvation.

17. Who cannot see, then, that salvation is the effect of faith? for as we have previously observed, all the heavenly beings work by this principle; and it is because they are able so to do that they are saved: for nothing but this could save them. And this is the lesson which the God of heaven, by the mouth of all his holy prophets, has been endeavoring to teach to the world. Hence we are told, that "without faith it is impossible to please God;" and that salvation is of faith, that it might be by grace to the end, the promise might be sure to all the seed. Romans 4:16. And that Israel, who followed after the law of righteousness, has not attained to the law of

righteousness. Wherefore? because they sought it not by faith, but as it were by the works of the law; for they stumbled at that stumbling stone. Romans 9:32. And Jesus said unto the man who brought his son to him, to get the devil who tormented him, cast out, "If thou canst believe, all things are possible to him that believeth." Mark 9:23. These with a multitude of other scriptures, which might be quoted, plainly set forth the light, in which the Savior, as well as the Former Day Saints, viewed the plan of salvation: That it was a system of faith—it begins with faith, and continues by faith; and every blessing which is obtained, in relation to it, is the effect of faith, whether it pertains to this life or that which is to come. To this all the revelations of God bear witness. If there were children of promise, they were the effects of faith: not even the Savior of the world excepted: "Blessed is she that believed," said Elizabeth to Mary, when she went to visit her; "for there shall be a performance of the things which where told her of the Lord;" Luke 1:45. Nor was the birth of John the Baptist the less a matter of faith; for in order that his father Zacharias might believe he was struck dumb. And through the whole history of the scheme of life and salvation, it is a matter of faith: every man received according to his faith: according as his faith was, so were his blessings and privileges; and nothing was withheld from him when his faith was sufficient to receive it. He could stop the mouths of lions, quench the violence of fire, escape the edge of the sword, wax valiant in fight, and put to flight the armies of the aliens; women could, by their faith, receive the dead children to life again: in a word, there was nothing impossible with them who had faith. All things were in subjection to the Former Day Saints, according as their faith was—By their faith they could obtain heavenly visions, the ministering of angels, have knowledge of the spirits of just men made perfect, of the general assembly and church of the first born, whose names are written in heaven, of God the judge of all, of Jesus the Mediator of the new covenant, and become familiar with the third heavens, see and hear things which were not only unutterable, but were unlawful to utter. Peter, in view of the power of faith, 2nd epistle, 1:1-3 says, to the Former Day Saints: "grace and peace be multiplied unto you, through the knowledge of God, and of Jesus our Lord, according as his divine power hath given unto us all things that pertain unto life and godliness, through the knowledge of him that has called us unto glory and virtue." In the first epistle, 1:3-5 he says, "Blessed be the God and Father of our Lord Jesus Christ, who according to his abundant mercy, has begotten us again unto a lively hope by the resurrection of Jesus Christ from the dead, to an inheritance incorruptible and undefiled, and that fadeth not away, reserved in heaven for you, who are kept by the power of God through faith unto salvation, ready to be revealed in the last time."

18. These sayings put together, show the Apostle's views, most clearly, so as to admit of no mistake on the mind of any individual. He says that all things that pertain to life and godliness were given unto them through the knowledge of God and our Savior Jesus Christ. And if the question is asked, how were they to obtain the knowledge of God? (for there is a great difference between believing in God and knowing him: knowledge implies more than faith. And notice, that all things that pertain to life and godliness, were given through the knowledge of God) the answer is given, through faith they were to obtain this knowledge; and having power by faith to obtain the knowledge of God, they could with it obtain all other things which pertain to life and godliness.

19. By these sayings of the Apostle we learn, that it was by obtaining a knowledge of God, that men got all things which pertain to life and godliness; and this knowledge was the effect

of faith. So that all things which pertain to life and godliness are the effects of faith.

20. From this we may extend as far as any circumstances may require whether on earth or in heaven, and we will find it the testimony of all inspired men, or heavenly messengers, that all things that pertain to life and godliness are the effects of faith and nothing else: all learning, wisdom, and prudence fail, and everything else as a means of salvation but faith. This is the reason that the fishermen of Galilee could teach the world—because they sought by faith and by faith obtained. And this is the reason that Paul counted all things but filth and dross—what he formerly called his gain he called his loss; yea, and he counted all things but loss for the excellency of the knowledge of Christ Jesus the Lord. Philippians 3:7-10: Because, to obtain the faith by which he could enjoy the knowledge of Christ Jesus the Lord, he had to suffer the loss of all things: this is the reason that the Former Day Saints knew more, and understood more of heaven, and of heavenly things than all others beside, because this information is the effect of faith-to be obtained by no other means. And this is the reason, that men, as soon as they lose their faith, run into strifes, contentions, darkness and difficulties; for the knowledge which tends to life disappears with faith, but returns when faith returns; for when faith comes, it brings its train of attendants with it—apostles, prophets, evangelists, pastors, teachers, gifts, wisdom, knowledge, miracles, healings, tongues, interpretation of tongues, etc. All these appear when faith appears on the earth, and disappear when it disappears from the earth. For these are the effects of faith and always have, and always will attend it. For where faith is, there will the knowledge of God be also, with all things which pertain thereto—revelations, visions, and dreams, as well as every other necessary thing in order that the possessors of faith may be perfected and obtain salvation; for God must change,

80

otherwise faith will prevail with him. And he who possesses it will, through it, obtain all necessary knowledge and wisdom until he shall know God, and the Lord Jesus Christ, whom he has sent: whom to know is eternal life: Amen.

KIRTLAND COLLAPSE/MISSOURI PERIL:
...IN PERILS AMONG FALSE BRETHREN

The foregoing *Lectures on Faith* were delivered in classes organized in Kirtland, Ohio. The classes were taught in the "School of the Prophets." The school name was a tribute to the Old Testament "sons of the prophets" (see, KJV 2 Kings 2) or "company of prophets" (see, RSV 2 Kings 2). The school used *Lectures* as their curriculum in the hope of developing students' faith. Joseph was unwilling to accept the failure of those first ordained to the high priesthood. He believed it was possible to produce people with faith like his own, those who would pierce the veil and commune with God. Joseph wanted to achieve something akin to Moses' accomplishment atop Mount Sinai when he, Aaron, Nadab, Abihu and seventy of the elders of Israel "saw the God of Israel." (See Exodus 24:9-10.)

Despite the initial failures, Joseph intended to produce other living witnesses of Christ's resurrection. He wanted to train those who could meet the New Testament requirement of an apostle. When Judas died, Matthias qualified to become an apostle because he was "a witness with [the other apostles] of his resurrection." (Acts 1:22.) Restoring the true religion would require true and living witnesses of Christ. The Gospel needed apostles, not just an old text written by apostles who had been dead for nearly two millennia. Christianity needed to live again.

On March 18, 1833, in a meeting of the School of the Prophets, a heavenly vision opened for some of those present. They saw God the Father and His Son Jesus Christ. The official minutes of the meeting include this brief mention: "many of the brethren saw a heavenly vision of the savior and concourses of angels." (*JS Papers, Documents, Vol. 3*, p. 42.) These results were exactly what Joseph hoped for from the *Lectures*. It suggested that if *some* believers could do it, then *anyone* could acquire the faith to do it.

After that appearance by Christ to the students of the School of the Prophets, Joseph declared to those who were witnesses of God the Father and Christ: "Brethren now you are prepared to be the Apostles of Jesus Christ, for you have seen both the Father and the Son, and know that They exist, and that They are two separate Personages." (*JS Papers, Documents, Vol. 3*, p. 43, footnote 259.) For the Mormon faith at that time, "apostleship" was not defined by membership in a "quorum," but by the witness a man had of the resurrected Christ. In all early Mormon records, notes, minutes and preaching prior to 1835 a man was an "apostle" because he witnessed Christ as a resurrected being.

The Church of Christ (as it was then named) was reorganized in 1835. Up to that time it had been a congregationalist church. Now a new multifaceted hierarchy was added atop existing local congregations. A traveling missionary order called the Quorum of Twelve Apostles was organized as one of the hierarchical bodies. Subsequently, the term "apostle" was redefined by Mormons to mean membership in that quorum. Today, all the splinter Mormon groups have "apostles" who belong to their sect's Quorum of the Twelve. It is no longer necessary to be a living witness of Christ's resurrection to be acknowledged as an apostle. The title has become office-based, requiring membership in that organizational group. Just like abandoning *Lectures on Faith*, Mormonism has abandoned the necessity of an apostle beholding Christ within the veil.

In addition to the traveling missionary apostles, a structure attempting to mimic the New Testament organization was created. This included a quorum of seventy, a presiding council of three high priests (a First Presidency) akin to the role of Peter, James and John in the Four Gospels, and local Bishops to preside over individual congregations. The various groups were originally considered "equal in authority" with each other. (D&C 107:24, 26, 36.) Equality among the groups was overthrown by the twelve apostles immediately following the death of Joseph Smith. Brigham Young abandoned the church government established by revelation through Joseph Smith and replaced it with an oligarchy of apostles. The apostles no longer traveled as missionaries, but became a standing board of directors controlling everything from budgets to personnel throughout LDS Mormonism. Breakaway factions have followed the LDS example.

In the first generation of Mormonism, Joseph called and ordained the members of the First Presidency. The Three Witnesses chose and ordained the original twelve apostles. The Seventy had Seven Presidents. These seven presidents selected the members of their quorum. The high council members were voted into their callings by their local congregations. Most importantly, any person could be voted out of any of these administrative offices at a conference by the members of the church. This included removing the president. In contrast to this democratic original, today the senior LDS apostle controls everything, and all offices are filled by a selection made from the top down. Although the church office names have remained the same since Joseph Smith, the functions and relationships within LDS Mormonism are now very different.

As the Mormon movement grew in the early 1830s, two population centers were established. There was one in Kirtland, Ohio and another in Independence, Missouri. In December, 1832 Joseph received a revelation requiring a temple to be built. The first temple was under construction in

Kirtland from 1832 until completed in March, 1836. The School of the Prophets met in that building.

By the time it was completed, incoming converts produced a strain on the local economy and, in turn, a capital shortage. In 1836, Joseph Smith helped form a bank that failed to obtain a state banking charter and therefore could not legally operate as a bank. It dropped "bank" from its name and was called the "Kirtland Safety Society." In January 1837 it began to issue notes that circulated as currency. Though not technically a bank, it operated exactly as a bank would, and investors likely did not regard it as anything else. By November of that year, the Safety Society, like hundreds of other banks, failed during a national banking crisis. The failure of the Kirtland Safety Society rocked the faith of many Mormons. Hostility grew, and within months dissidents attempted to take possession of the temple and control of the church.

Troubles increased over the next two years for Joseph Smith until he was faced with seemingly insurmountable challenges. His catastrophe began the year before when he was at the helm of the failed Kirtland Safety Society. Loyal Mormons were led to believe the bank was founded on inspiration and was therefore watched over by God. Warren Parrish, the Kirtland Safety Society bank cashier and one-time scribe and secretary for Joseph Smith, left the faith over the Safety Society failure. He published a letter in a local newspaper claiming the following: "I have listened to him [i.e. Smith] with feelings of no ordinary kind, when he declared that the audible voice of God, instructed him to establish a banking-anti banking institution, who like Aaron's rod shall swallow up all other banks (the Bank of Monroe excepted,) and grow and flourish and spread from the rivers to the ends of the earth, and survive when all others should be laid in ruins." (*Painesville Republican*, February 22, 1838.)

Loyal Mormon (later LDS Church president) Wilford Woodruff likewise confirmed the bank was founded upon God's direction given through Joseph Smith. He recorded in his journal, "I also herd [sic] President Joseph Smith, jr., declare in the presence of F. Williams, D. Whitmer, S. Smith, W. Parrish, and others in the Deposit office that he had received that morning the word of the Lord upon the subject of the Kirtland Safety Society. He was alone in a room by himself and he had not only [heard] the voice of the Spirit upon the Subject but even an audible voice. He did not tell us at that time what the Lord said upon the subject but remarked that if we would give heed to the commandments the Lord had given this morning all would be well." (*Wilford Woodruff's Journal*, January 6, 1837.)

The Panic of 1837 began in May, and resulted in the failure of over half the banks in the United States. On May 10 of that year, New York chartered banks stopped paying in gold and silver coinage, and ill-liquid institutions like the Kirtland Safety Society were unable to survive the panic. Demands on the institution were impossible to satisfy, and like many other institutions, it went out of business.

The image of the Kirtland Safety Society was already tarnished by the failure to obtain a bank charter. It issued printed bills using the word "banking" preceded by "Anti" to reflect the lack of a bank charter. Most who trusted the institution did so because of their religious confidence in Joseph Smith. When it failed, many lost not only their money, but also their confidence in Joseph. In July 1837, the Kirtland Safety Society closed its doors. By late 1837 the church in Kirtland was in complete turmoil. Several hundred saints questioned Joseph Smith's divine calling as they left the church. A number of angry dissidents tried to seize leadership of the church. They wanted Joseph voted out of office and driven from Kirtland.

Joining the disaffected leader Warren Parrish, were three apostles of the church, John F. Boynton, and Luke and Wyman Johnson. Seventies quorum members Hasten Aldridge, Leonard Ridge, Sylvester Smith, John Gould, John Grayson, and Martin Harris, one of the Three Witnesses to the *Book of Mormon*, abandoned Joseph. The church Joseph founded was in disarray.

In January 1838, Joseph Smith had a revelation saying in part, "Thus saith the Lord, Let the presidency of my Church take their families as soon as practical, and the door is open for them and move on to the west as fast as the way is made plain before their faces and let their hearts be comforted for I will be with them." That very night (January 12, 1838), Joseph Smith and Sidney Rigdon fled Kirtland under cover of darkness. They were chased for 200 miles by an angry mob comprised largely of disaffected Mormons. The mob included members who had suffered significant financial losses as a result of the bank failure. They were intent on taking Joseph's life as an act of revenge. January 1838 began another terrible year.

As a result of an earlier revelation given in March 1831, John Whitmer was chosen by the Lord to be the historian for the church. His original appointment stated, *"Behold, it is expedient in me that my servant John...* [John Whitmer, one of the Eight Witnesses to the *Book of Mormon*, brother of David Whitmer, who was in turn one of the Three Witnesses.] *...should write and keep a regular history, and assist you, my servant Joseph, in transcribing all things which shall be given you, until he is called to further duties."* (D&C 47:1.) On March 8, 1831, and for the succeeding seven years, the history of the church had been compiled and maintained by John Whitmer. He had the record of the expulsion of the saints from Jackson County in 1833. He recorded Zion's Camp in 1834. He recorded the 1837 collapse of the Kirtland Safety Society and the ensuing rebellion, the apostasy of Kirtland members, nighttime flight of Joseph and Sidney, and their relocation to Missouri. When Whitmer's history was lost, the record of the first seven years of Mormonism was also lost.

The loss of Kirtland was just a beginning of the second great setback. Like the earlier failed priesthood ordinations, once again it seemed Joseph had only grandiose pretentions that failed to materialize into any benefit for his followers.

Joseph's flight to Missouri brought neither safety nor an end to Mormon dissent. The Kirtland citizens may have been enraged by the bank failure, but Missouri was also a hotbed of discontent and criticism.

During these same years, as the temple was being built in Kirtland, Mormons were gathering in Missouri, expecting to see a New Jerusalem built there. The rapidly increasing Missouri Mormon population antagonized the Missouri locals. The end of 1833 erupted in violence between the two communities. Joseph's followers were driven out of the city of Independence and then out of Jackson County. Mormons were compelled to relocate to a new county organized in the sparsely populated Missouri north. Kirtland had a temple, but Independence was where the future Zion was expected to rise. Most of the believers originally migrated to Jackson County, Missouri, hoping to live in God's New Jerusalem.

Work on the Kirtland temple was interrupted for three months beginning May 1834 while Joseph led a group of Mormons to Missouri. This was called "Zion's Camp." It was an abortive attempt to restore displaced Mormons to their Jackson County property. The march terminated without an armed conflict. Displaced Missouri Mormons were unable to return to Jackson County.

Mormon leaders W.W. Phelps and church historian John Whitmer founded the city of Far West in 1836 where many Mormon refugees regrouped. A three-man presidency of

David Whitmer, Oliver Cowdery and W.W. Phelps was established to preside over the Mormon society in Missouri.

Joseph's difficulties increased early in 1838 when rumor began circulating among the Missouri Mormons of immoral conduct by Joseph Smith. Joseph's former close friend and *Book of Mormon* scribe, Oliver Cowdery was the source of the accusation. Cowdery's insinuations resulted in a church court held April 12, 1838 by the Far West High Council. A total of nine charges were brought against Cowdery. At the time, Cowdery was the Assistant President to the Church and respected as the "second elder" of the church. Cowdery had been one of the Three Witnesses to the *Book of Mormon* and had selected and ordained the church's first Twelve Apostles. The trial was perhaps the most significant to be held in the history of the church.

The charges against Cowdery included the following: "For seeking to destroy the character of President Joseph Smith Junior by falsely insinuating that he was guilty of adultery etc." After taking evidence, the High Council ultimately ex-communicated Oliver Cowdery and cleared Joseph of the charge. The minutes of the High Council said they dealt with "the girl business," meaning Oliver's allegations against Joseph. Joseph was exonerated. (See Donald Q. Cannon and Lyndon W. Cook, eds., *Far West Record: Minutes of the Church of Jesus Christ of Latter-day Saints*, 1830-1844 (Salt Lake City: Deseret Book Co., 1983), 162-163.) The un-substantiated charge that Joseph was an adulterer has remained with Mormonism, moving from rumor, to formal accusation, and finally into history. Today, essentially every Mormon sect either reluctantly admits, or vigorously advocates that plural wives originated with Joseph Smith. The closer the historical record is examined, however, the less evidence there appears to support Joseph as the originator, and the more evidence there is to implicate

Brigham Young. Brigham Young publicly advocated the practice. Joseph denounced it publicly and excommunicated those who he found engaged in it.

David Whitmer, another of the Three Witnesses, also left the church in 1838 but was not formally excommunicated. His brother John Whitmer, the church historian, was excommunicated and took the history with him, refusing to return it to Joseph. Prominent and respected Mormons Hiram Page (one of the Eight Witnesses) and W.W. Phelps (a member of the high council) also left the church in 1838.

On July 4, 1838 Sidney Rigdon delivered an infamous "Salt Sermon," warning that dissenters were worthy of being "trodden, like salt that lost its savor" under the feet of the saints. Because of the talk, Joseph's former close friends and church leaders Oliver Cowdery, David Whitmer, John Whitmer, W.W. Phelps and Lyman E. Johnson were warned to leave Far West or face "a fatal calamity." Friends were now enemies. Joseph's people divided into turmoil. In response to the threats against these men, everybody but Phelps fled.

Rigdon's Salt Sermon did not just threaten disaffected Mormons. He also threatened a "war of extermination" against the non-Mormons of Missouri if they didn't stop annoying the Mormons. The threats ignited anti-Mormon opposition. It prompted many of the disaffected Mormons, including leaders, to change sides and join the Missouri mobs. These former leaders used their credibility as insiders to incite greater anger and hostility toward the church. The animosities soon turned into armed conflict and arson. Missourians believed Mormons threatened them. Mormons thought they were acting in defense, and justified their own violence as "defending" themselves. In response to the outbreak of hostility between Mormons and Missourians, in October 1838, Missouri Governor Lilburn Boggs issued an "Extermination Order" directing that Mormons be slain or driven from the State of Missouri. The Order gave violence against Mormons legitimacy and made Mormon responses an act of war against the state. The resulting conflict has become known as "The Mormon War."

Former Mormon leaders signed affidavits accusing Joseph Smith and his church organization of criminal and moral wrongdoing. Thomas Marsh, president of the Quorum of the Twelve Apostles, signed an affidavit on October 24, 1838 condemning Joseph. The Marsh allegations were endorsed by a second affidavit from fellow apostle Orson Hyde. The Marsh affidavit was signed the same day open warfare commenced and said in part that "Joseph Smith, the Prophet, had preached [at Far West]…that all the Mormons who refused to take up arms, if necessary, in difficulties with the citizens, should be shot, or otherwise put to death[.]" The implication was that Joseph Smith was responsible for the Mormon violence directed at Missouri citizens.

After recounting circumstantial evidence of thefts by Mormons he claimed were supervised by Joseph, the Marsh affidavit stated,

> They have among them a company consisting of all that are considered true Mormons, called the Danites, who have taken an oath to support the heads of the Church in all things, that they say or do, whether right or wrong. … On Saturday last, I am informed by the Mormons that they had a meeting at Far West, at which they appointed a company of twelve, by the name of the Destruction Company, for the purpose of burning and destroying; … they passed a decree that no Mormon dissenter should leave Caldwell county alive; and that such as attempted to do it, should be shot down, and sent to tell their tale in eternity. In a conversation between Dr. Avard

and other Mormons, said Avard proposed to start a pestilence among the Gentiles, as he called them, by poisoning their corn, fruit, &c., and saying it was the work of the Lord; and said Avard advocated lying for the support of their religion, and said it was no harm to lie for the Lord!! The plan of said Smith, the Prophet, is to take this State; and he professes to his people to intend taking the United States, and ultimately the whole world. This is the belief of the Church, and my own opinion of the Prophet's plans and intentions. It is my opinion that neither said Joseph Smith, the Prophet, nor any one of the principal men, who is firm in the faith, could be indicted for any offense in the county of Caldwell. The Prophet inculcates the notion, and it is believed by every true Mormon that Smith's prophecies are superior to the law of the land. I have heard the Prophet say that he should yet tread down his enemies, and walk over their dead bodies; that if he was not let alone, he would be a second Mahomet [Mohammad] to this generation, and that he would make it one gore of blood from the Rocky Mountains to the Atlantic Ocean; that like Mahomet, whose motto, is treating for peace, was "Al Koran or the Sword," so should it be eventually with us, "Joseph Smith or the Sword." These last statements were made during the last summer.

Later, in calmer times, both Marsh and Hyde would recant their sworn affidavits. But in 1838 their statements provided justification for the Missouri political leaders, militia and general population to see Joseph Smith and Mormons as a clear and present danger to them and their property.

A Man Without Doubt

The first skirmishes between Mormons and Missourians began in August 1838 at a polling station when Mormons tried to vote. A band of Mormons led by Sampson Avard confronted election judge Adam Black about the failure to protect Mormon voting rights. Joseph Smith was among these Mormons. Judge Black attributed threats of violence to Avard, but said Joseph did not approve and instead possessed no such heart for violence. In the aftermath of the polling station fight, Avard's authority to direct the Mormon militia was taken and he was reassigned as a surgeon. The reassignment was because Joseph did not want violence to be used to resolve conflicts and Avard thought otherwise. Avard testified in November 1828, "I once had a command as an officer, but Joseph Smith, jr., removed me from it, and I asked him the reason, and he assigned that he had another office for me. Afterwards Mr. Rigdon told me I was to fill the office of surgeon, to attend to the sick and wounded." (Testimony before Judge Austin A. King, 5th District Court of Missouri, November 12, 1838.)

Avard continued to support violence against perceived enemies, and formed a group that came to be known as the "Danites." Joseph denied he approved or supported Avard's group or violent actions. Historians have debated the question of Joseph's involvement with the Danite organization and activities. Joseph's denials have been questioned largely because of testimony against Joseph given by Avard in 1838.

While Avard was acting in the role of a surgeon, the battle of Crooked River was fought on October 24, 1838. The Extermination Order was issued on October 27, 1838. Three days later, October 30, 1838 at Haun's Mill, the Missouri Militia, led by Colonel William Jennings, Sheriff of Livingston County, massacred a group of Mormons. Some even after they surrendered. None of the Missouri Militia was killed. The Mormon dead totaled at least 17, including a 78 year-old

Revolutionary War veteran, whose body was decapitated and dismembered after he had surrendered. The militia also killed two boys, ages 9 and 10.

Joseph Smith surrendered at the city of Far West while it was under siege. On November 1st he was sentenced to death "at 9 o'clock tomorrow morning in a public square at Far West."

Following the mob troubles in Kirtland, Ohio and Missouri, and in the months prior to his surrender at Far West, Joseph Smith began to compose a replacement history for the one John Whitmer took with him. Joseph Smith, against some of the greatest opposition, treachery, betrayal, confusion and violence he would endure, composed his history. Contrary to the events immediately before he commenced writing, his history is filled with optimism, faith and testimony. He relates the earliest events of his encounter with God in a new light. Instead of a personal conversion, it became God's approach to all mankind by commissioning Joseph Smith to testify of Him and restore lost parts of the true religion.

He describes the events from 1820 to 1829 primarily as they relate to restoring the Gospel of Christ. If the account is viewed only as a history of those nine years it has one meaning—addressing the Christian community. But if it is read as a reflection of the preceding three years, it has another more probable meaning: It is addressing Mormon dissidents. Joseph's testimony did not indict childhood persecutors, but denounced the church's dissidents who should have known better. Their misconduct mirrored the earlier opposition he encountered in his youth. His youthful persecutors were only verbally abusive. His 1838 opponents were out for blood. The Mormons were far more dangerous and threatening to him than the Christians of his youth. LDS Mormons never see themselves as the ones condemned in his history. But it was them he was addressing; much more so than the neighbors he had as a lad in 1820.

Joseph Smith's history of the church begins with his birth in 1805. Then moves quickly to retell the religious excitement of 1820, and his sincere confusion about which church to join. He found an answer in the *Bible*, which recommended he ask God. He asked, God answered, and Joseph was given "a work to do."

His replacement history made it clear he was not performing his own errand, but acting according to God's direction. Those who thought him deluded, both in his childhood and in 1838, "should have endeavored in a kind and affectionate manner to reclaim him." They had not done so either time, and now the dissident Mormons were cast into the role filled earlier by his Protestant persecutors.

Of all the accounts Joseph Smith gave of his First Vision of God, ironically it is the 1838 version that was adopted by the LDS as Mormon scripture. It was composed in the worst of times, under the worst of circumstances. It indicts faithless followers who were, and still are, oblivious to Joseph's criticism of Mormons.

Even as others he trusted disbelieved and denounced him, Joseph Smith remained confident of his divine calling. The 1838 version is a product and proof of Joseph's faith. He defended all he had been through, and composed an account of his experiences that reaffirmed God's central role in his life.

Joseph Smith's original written 1838 history has been lost and no copy survives. The *Joseph Smith Papers*, now published by the LDS Church Historian's Office, provides the earliest version copied in 1839. That document is a handwritten copy by James Mulholland, Joseph's secretary at the time. The Mulholland version is the one used in the *Joseph Smith History* account of the volume of Mormon scripture titled *The Pearl of*

Great Price. It is believed to be a faithful copy of the 1838 document because of its internal dating. In the second verse it recounts: "...being now [1838] the eighth year since the organization of the said Church." Mulholland apparently copied Joseph's account faithfully in 1839, and preserved its internal dating from the prior year.

The opening words of Joseph's history were written because of the events of 1837 and 1838. It is his response to formerly faithful Mormons. Their anger and rejection of him gives the context for the opening verse. *"Owing to the many reports which have been put in circulation by evil-disposed and designing persons, in relation to the rise and progress of the Church of Jesus Christ of Latter-day Saints,"* These false reports did not originate with non-Mormons. It was the lies, the hostile accusations, and affidavits from disaffected Mormons, church apostles, seventies, High Council members, the Three Witnesses, and others who left the church. His close associates and pretended friends abandoned him. As great religious figures often do, Joseph explained the events using his faith in God contrasted with "evil-disposed" opponents. It is the eternal conflict between faith and faithlessness, good and evil, obedience to God and rebellion against heaven. These are the overarching reasons for his difficulties. His faith emerges with clarity, and with inspiring words summoned to defend his understanding of God's role in his life.

"In this history I shall present the various events in relation to this Church, in truth and righteousness, as they have transpired, or as they at present exist, being now [1838] the eighth year since the organization of the said Church."

The history was composed in 1838. It tells his story using events that happened eighteen years earlier. The account, however, directly responded to the crisis of faith underway among followers in 1837-1838. Mormonism was teetering, but

A Man Without Doubt

Joseph stood firm and reaffirmed he was called by God and doing His work.

JOSEPH SMITH HISTORY
BY JOSEPH SMITH
...IN WATCHINGS OFTEN

Owing to the many reports which have been put in circulation by evil-disposed and designing persons, in relation to the rise and progress of the Church of Jesus Christ of Latter-day Saints, all of which have been designed by the authors thereof to militate against its character as a Church and its progress in the world—I have been induced to write this history, to disabuse the public mind, and put all inquirers after truth in possession of the facts, as they have transpired, in relation both to myself and the Church, so far as I have such facts in my possession.

In this history I shall present the various events in relation to this Church, in truth and righteousness, as they have transpired, or as they at present exist, being now [1838] the eighth year since the organization of the said Church.

I was born in the year of our Lord one thousand eight hundred and five, on the twenty-third day of December, in the town of Sharon, Windsor county, State of Vermont. ... My father, Joseph Smith, Sen., left the State of Vermont, and moved to Palmyra, Ontario (now Wayne) county, in the State of New York, when I was in my tenth year, or thereabouts. In about four years after my father's arrival in Palmyra, he moved with his family into Manchester in the same county of Ontario—

His family consisting of eleven souls, namely, my father, Joseph Smith; my mother, Lucy Smith (whose name, previous to her marriage, was Mack, daughter of Solomon Mack); my brothers, Alvin (who died November 19th, 1823, in the 26th year of his age), Hyrum, myself, Samuel Harrison, William, Don Carlos; and my sisters, Sophronia, Catherine, and Lucy.

Some time in the second year after our removal to Manchester, there was in the place where we lived an unusual excitement on the subject of religion. It commenced with the Methodists, but soon became general among all the sects in that region of country. Indeed, the whole district of country seemed affected by it, and great multitudes united themselves to the different religious parties, which created no small stir and division amongst the people, some crying, "Lo, here!" and others, "Lo, there!" Some were contending for the Methodist faith, some for the Presbyterian, and some for the Baptist.

For, notwithstanding the great love which the converts to these different faiths expressed at the time of their conversion, and the great zeal manifested by the respective clergy, who were active in getting up and promoting this extraordinary scene of religious feeling, in order to have everybody converted, as they were pleased to call it, let them join what sect they pleased; yet when the converts began to file off, some to one party and some to another, it was seen that the seemingly good feelings of both the priests and the converts were more pretended than real; for a scene of great confusion and bad feeling ensued—priest contending against priest, and convert against convert; so that all their good feelings one for another, if they ever had any, were entirely lost in a strife of words and a contest about opinions.

I was at this time in my fifteenth year. My father's family was proselyted to the Presbyterian faith, and four of them joined that church, namely, my mother, Lucy; my brothers Hyrum and Samuel Harrison; and my sister Sophronia.

During this time of great excitement my mind was called up to serious reflection and great uneasiness; but though my feelings were deep and often poignant, still I kept myself aloof from all these parties, though I attended their several meetings as often as occasion would permit. In process of time my mind became somewhat partial to the Methodist sect, and I felt some desire to be united with them; but so great were the confusion and strife among the different denominations, that it was impossible for a person young as I was, and so unacquainted with men and things, to come to any certain conclusion who was right and who was wrong.

My mind at times was greatly excited, the cry and tumult were so great and incessant. The Presbyterians were most decided against the Baptists and Methodists, and used all the powers of both reason and sophistry to prove their errors, or, at least, to make the people think they were in error. On the other hand, the Baptists and Methodists in their turn were equally zealous in endeavoring to establish their own tenets and disprove all others.

In the midst of this war of words and tumult of opinions, I often said to myself: What is to be done? Who of all these parties are right; or, are they all wrong together? If any one of them be right, which is it, and how shall I know it?

While I was laboring under the extreme difficulties caused by the contests of these parties of religionists, I was one day reading the Epistle of James, first chapter and fifth verse, which reads: *If any of you lack wisdom, let him ask of God, that giveth to all men liberally, and upbraideth not; and it shall be given him.*

Never did any passage of scripture come with more power to the heart of man than this did at this time to mine. It seemed to enter with great force into every feeling of my heart. I reflected on it again and again, knowing that if any person needed wisdom from God, I did; for how to act I did not know, and unless I could get more wisdom than I then had, I would never know; for the teachers of religion of the different sects understood the same passages of scripture so differently as to destroy all confidence in settling the question by an appeal to the Bible.

At length I came to the conclusion that I must either remain in darkness and confusion, or else I must do as James directs, that is, ask of God. I at length came to the determination to "ask of God," concluding that if he gave wisdom to them that lacked wisdom, and would give liberally, and not upbraid, I might venture.

So, in accordance with this, my determination to ask of God, I retired to the woods to make the attempt. It was on the morning of a beautiful, clear day, early in the spring of eighteen hundred and twenty. It was the first time in my life that I had made such an attempt, for amidst all my anxieties I had never as yet made the attempt to pray vocally.

After I had retired to the place where I had previously designed to go, having looked around me, and finding myself alone, I kneeled down and began to offer up the desires of my heart to God. I had scarcely done so, when immediately I was seized upon by some power which entirely overcame me, and had such an astonishing influence over me as to bind my tongue so that I could not speak. Thick darkness gathered around me, and it seemed to me for a time as if I were doomed to sudden destruction.

But, exerting all my powers to call upon God to deliver me out of the power of this enemy which had seized upon me, and at the very moment when I was ready to sink into despair and abandon myself to destruction—not to an imaginary ruin, but to the power of some actual being from the unseen world, who had such marvelous power as I had never before felt in any being—just at this moment of great alarm, I saw a pillar of light exactly over my head, above the brightness of the sun, which descended gradually until it fell upon me.

It no sooner appeared than I found myself delivered from the enemy which held me bound. When the light rested upon me I saw two Personages, whose brightness and glory defy all description, standing above me in the air. One of them spake unto me, calling me by name and said, pointing to the other— *This is My Beloved Son. Hear Him!*

My object in going to inquire of the Lord was to know which of all the sects was right, that I might know which to join. No sooner, therefore, did I get possession of myself, so as to be able to speak, than I asked the Personages who stood above me in the light, which of all the sects was right (for at this time it had never entered into my heart that all were wrong)—and which I should join.

I was answered that I must join none of them, for they were all wrong; and the Personage who addressed me said that all their creeds were an abomination in his sight; that those professors were all corrupt; that: "they draw near to me with their lips, but their hearts are far from me, they teach for doctrines the commandments of men, having a form of godliness, but they deny the power thereof."

He again forbade me to join with any of them; and many other things did he say unto me, which I cannot write at this time. When I came to myself again, I found myself lying on my back, looking up into heaven. When the light had departed, I had no strength; but soon recovering in some degree, I went home. And as I leaned up to the fireplace, mother inquired what the matter was. I replied, "Never mind, all is well—I am well enough off." I then said to my mother, "I have learned for myself that Presbyterianism is not true."

It seems as though the adversary was aware, at a very early period of my life, that I was destined to prove a disturber and an annoyer of his kingdom; else why should the powers of darkness combine against me? Why the opposition and persecution that arose against me, almost in my infancy?

Some few days after I had this vision, I happened to be in company with one of the Methodist preachers, who was very active in the before mentioned religious excitement; and, conversing with him on the subject of religion, I took occasion to give him an account of the vision which I had had. I was greatly surprised at his behavior; he treated my communication not only lightly, but with great contempt, saying it was all of the devil, that there were no such things as visions or revelations in these days; that all such things had ceased with the apostles, and that there would never be any more of them.

I soon found, however, that my telling the story had excited a great deal of prejudice against me among professors of religion, and was the cause of great persecution, which continued to increase; and though I was an obscure boy, only between fourteen and fifteen years of age, and my circumstances in life such as to make a boy of no consequence in the world, yet men of high standing would take notice sufficient to excite the public mind against me, and create a bitter persecution; and this was common among all the sects—all united to persecute me.

It caused me serious reflection then, and often has since, how very strange it was that an obscure boy, of a little over fourteen years of age, and one, too, who was doomed to the necessity of obtaining a scanty maintenance by his daily labor, should be thought a character of sufficient importance to attract the attention of the great ones of the most popular sects of the day, and in a manner to create in them a spirit of the most bitter persecution and reviling. But strange or not, so it was, and it was often the cause of great sorrow to myself.

However, it was nevertheless a fact that I had beheld a vision. I have thought since, that I felt much like Paul, when he made his defense before King Agrippa, and related the account of the vision he had when he saw a light, and heard a voice; but still there were but few who believed him; some said he was dishonest, others said he was mad; and he was ridiculed and reviled. But all this did not destroy the reality of his vision. He had seen a vision, he knew he had, and all the persecution under heaven could not make it otherwise; and though they should persecute him unto death, yet he knew, and would know to his latest breath, that he had both seen a light and heard a voice speaking unto him, and all the world could not make him think or believe otherwise.

So it was with me. I had actually seen a light, and in the midst of that light I saw two Personages, and they did in reality speak to me; and though I was hated and persecuted for saying that I had seen a vision, yet it was true;

105

and while they were persecuting me, reviling me, and speaking all manner of evil against me falsely for so saying, I was led to say in my heart: Why persecute me for telling the truth? I have actually seen a vision; and who am I that I can withstand God, or why does the world think to make me deny what I have actually seen? For I had seen a vision; I knew it, and I knew that God knew it, and I could not deny it, neither dared I do it; at least I knew that by so doing I would offend God, and come under condemnation.

I had now got my mind satisfied so far as the sectarian world was concerned—that it was not my duty to join with any of them, but to continue as I was until further directed. I had found the testimony of James to be true—that a man who lacked wisdom might ask of God, and obtain, and not be upbraided.

I continued to pursue my common vocations in life until the twenty-first of September, one thousand eight hundred and twenty-three, all the time suffering severe persecution at the hands of all classes of men, both religious and irreligious, because I continued to affirm that I had seen a vision.

During the space of time which intervened between the time I had the vision and the year eighteen hundred and twenty-three—having been forbidden to join any of the religious sects of the day, and being of very tender years, and persecuted by those who ought to have been my friends and to have treated me kindly, and if they supposed me to be deluded to have endeavored in a proper and affectionate manner to have reclaimed me—I was left to all kinds of temptations; and, mingling with all kinds of society, I frequently fell into many foolish errors, and displayed the weakness of youth, and the foibles of human nature; which, I am sorry to say, led me into divers temptations, offensive in the sight of God. In making this confession, no one need suppose me guilty of any great or malignant sins. A disposition to commit such was never in my nature. But I was guilty of levity, and sometimes associated with jovial company, etc., not consistent with that character which ought to be maintained by one who was called of God as I had been. But this will not seem very strange to anyone who recollects my youth, and is acquainted with my native cheery temperament.

In consequence of these things, I often felt condemned for my weakness and imperfections; when, on the evening of the above-mentioned twenty-first of September, after I had retired to my bed for the night, I betook myself to prayer and supplication to Almighty God for forgiveness of all my sins and follies, and also for a manifestation to me, that I might know of my state and standing before him; for I had full confidence in obtaining a divine manifestation, as I previously had one.

While I was thus in the act of calling upon God, I discovered a light appearing in my room, which continued to increase until the room was lighter than at noonday, when immediately a personage appeared at my bedside, standing in the air, for his feet did not touch the floor.

He had on a loose robe of most exquisite whiteness. It was a whiteness beyond anything earthly I had ever seen; nor do I believe that any earthly thing could be made to appear so exceedingly white and brilliant. His hands were naked, and his arms also, a little above the wrist; so, also, were his feet naked, as were his legs, a little above the ankles. His head and neck were also bare. I could discover that he had no other clothing on but this robe, as it was open, so that I could see into his bosom.

Not only was his robe exceedingly white, but his whole person was glorious beyond description, and his countenance truly like lightning. The room was exceedingly light, but not so very bright as immediately around his person. When I first looked upon him, I was afraid; but the fear soon left me.

He called me by name, and said unto me that he was a messenger sent from the presence of God to me, and that his name was Moroni; that God had a work for me to do; and that my name should be had for good and evil among all nations, kindreds, and tongues, or that it should be both good and evil spoken of among all people.

He said there was a book deposited, written upon gold plates, giving an account of the former inhabitants of this continent, and the source from whence they sprang. He also said that the fulness of the everlasting Gospel was contained in it, as delivered by the Savior to the ancient inhabitants;

Also, that there were two stones in silver bows—and these stones, fastened to a breastplate, constituted what is called the Urim and Thummim—deposited with the plates; and the possession and use of these stones were what constituted "seers" in ancient or former times; and that God had prepared them for the purpose of translating the book.

After telling me these things, he commenced quoting the prophecies of the Old Testament. He first quoted part of the third chapter of Malachi; and he quoted also the fourth or last chapter of the same prophecy, though with a little variation from the way it reads in our Bible. Instead of quoting the first verse as it reads in our books, he quoted it thus:

"*For behold, the day cometh that shall burn as an oven, and all the proud, yea, and all that do wickedly shall burn as stubble; for they that come shall burn them, saith the Lord of Hosts, that it shall leave them neither root nor branch.*"

And again, he quoted the fifth verse thus:

"*Behold, I will reveal unto you the Priesthood, by the hand of Elijah the prophet, before the coming of the great and dreadful day of the Lord.*"

He also quoted the next verse differently:

"*And he shall plant in the hearts of the children the promises made to the fathers, and the hearts of the children shall turn to their fathers. If it were not so, the whole earth would be utterly wasted at his coming.*"

In addition to these, he quoted the eleventh chapter of Isaiah, saying that it was about to be fulfilled. He quoted also the third chapter of Acts, twenty-second and twenty-third verses, precisely as they stand in our New Testament. He said that that prophet was Christ; but the day had not yet come when "they who would not hear his voice should be cut off from among the people," but soon would come.

He also quoted the second chapter of Joel, from the twenty-eighth verse to the last. He also said that this was not yet fulfilled, but was soon to be. And he further stated that the fulness of the Gentiles was soon to come in. He quoted many other passages of scripture, and offered many explanations which cannot be mentioned here.

Again, he told me, that when I got those plates of which he had spoken—for the time that they should be obtained was not yet fulfilled—I should not show them to any person; neither the breastplate with the Urim and Thummim; only to those to whom I should be commanded to show them; if I did I should be destroyed. While he was conversing with me about the plates, the vision was opened to my mind that I could see the place where the plates were deposited, and that so clearly and distinctly that I knew the place again when I visited it.

After this communication, I saw the light in the room begin to gather immediately around the person of him who had been speaking to me, and it continued to do so until the room was again left dark, except just around him; when, instantly I saw, as it were, a conduit open right up into heaven, and he ascended till he entirely disappeared, and the room was left as it had been before this heavenly light had made its appearance.

I lay musing on the singularity of the scene, and marveling greatly at what had been told to me by this extraordinary messenger; when, in the midst of my meditation, I suddenly discovered that my room was again beginning to get lighted, and in an instant, as it were, the same heavenly messenger was again by my bedside.

He commenced, and again related the very same things which he had done at his first visit, without the least variation; which having done, he informed me of great judgments which were coming upon the earth, with great desolations by famine, sword, and pestilence; and that these grievous judgments would come on the earth in this generation. Having related these things, he again ascended as he had done before.

By this time, so deep were the impressions made on my mind, that sleep had fled from my eyes, and I lay overwhelmed in astonishment at what I had both seen and heard. But what was my surprise when again I beheld the same messenger at my bedside, and heard him rehearse or repeat over again to me the same things as before; and added a caution to me, telling me that Satan would try to tempt me (in consequence of the indigent circumstances of my father's family), to get the plates for the purpose of getting rich. This he forbade me, saying that I must have no other object in view in getting the plates but to glorify God, and must not be influenced by any other motive than that of building his kingdom; otherwise I could not get them.

After this third visit, he again ascended into heaven as before, and I was again left to ponder on the strangeness of what I had just experienced; when almost immediately after the heavenly messenger had ascended from me for the third time, the cock crowed, and I found that day was approaching, so that our interviews must have occupied the whole of that night.

I shortly after arose from my bed, and, as usual, went to the necessary labors of the day; but, in attempting to work as at other times, I found my strength so exhausted as to render me entirely unable. My father, who was laboring along with me, discovered something to be wrong with me, and told me to go home. I started with the intention of going to the house; but, in attempting to cross the fence out of the field where we were, my strength entirely failed me, and I fell helpless on the ground, and for a time was quite unconscious of anything.

The first thing that I can recollect was a voice speaking unto me, calling me by name. I looked up, and beheld the same messenger standing over my head, surrounded by light as before. He then again related unto me all that he had related to me the previous night, and commanded me to go to my father and tell him of the vision and commandments which I had received.

I obeyed; I returned to my father in the field, and rehearsed the whole matter to him. He replied to me that it was of God, and told me to go and do as commanded by the messenger. I left the field, and went to the place where the messenger had told me the plates were deposited; and owing to the distinctness of the vision which I had had concerning it, I knew the place the instant that I arrived there.

Convenient to the village of Manchester, Ontario county, New York, stands a hill of considerable size, and the most elevated of any in the neighborhood. On the west side of this hill, not far from the top, under a stone of considerable size, lay the plates, deposited in a stone box. This stone was thick and rounding in the middle on the upper side, and thinner towards the edges, so that the middle part of it was visible above the ground, but the edge all around was covered with earth.

Having removed the earth, I obtained a lever, which I got fixed under the edge of the stone, and with a little exertion raised it up. I looked in, and there indeed did I behold the plates, the Urim and Thummim, and the breastplate, as stated by the messenger. The box in which they lay was formed by laying stones together in some kind of cement. In the bottom of the box were laid two stones crossways of the box, and on these stones lay the plates and the other things with them.

I made an attempt to take them out, but was forbidden by the messenger, and was again informed that the time for bringing them forth had not yet arrived, neither would it, until four years from that time; but he told me that I should come to that place precisely in one year from that time, and that he

112

would there meet with me, and that I should continue to do so until the time should come for obtaining the plates.

Accordingly, as I had been commanded, I went at the end of each year, and at each time I found the same messenger there, and received instruction and intelligence from him at each of our interviews, respecting what the Lord was going to do, and how and in what manner his kingdom was to be conducted in the last days.

As my father's worldly circumstances were very limited, we were under the necessity of laboring with our hands, hiring out by day's work and otherwise, as we could get opportunity. Sometimes we were at home, and sometimes abroad, and by continuous labor were enabled to get a comfortable maintenance.

In the year 1823 my father's family met with a great affliction by the death of my eldest brother, Alvin. In the month of October, 1825, I hired with an old gentleman by the name of Josiah Stoal, who lived in Chenango county, State of New York. He had heard something of a silver mine having been opened by the Spaniards in Harmony, Susquehanna county, State of Pennsylvania; and had, previous to my hiring to him, been digging, in order, if possible, to discover the mine. After I went to live with him, he took me, with the rest of his hands, to dig for the silver mine, at which I continued to work for nearly a month, without success in our undertaking, and finally I prevailed with the old gentleman to cease digging after it. Hence arose the very prevalent story of my having been a money-digger.

During the time that I was thus employed, I was put to board with a Mr. Isaac Hale, of that place; it was there I first saw my wife (his daughter), Emma Hale. On the 18th of

January, 1827, we were married, while I was yet employed in the service of Mr. Stoal.

Owing to my continuing to assert that I had seen a vision, persecution still followed me, and my wife's father's family were very much opposed to our being married. I was, therefore, under the necessity of taking her elsewhere; so we went and were married at the house of Squire Tarbill, in South Bainbridge, Chenango county, New York. Immediately after my marriage, I left Mr. Stoal's, and went to my father's, and farmed with him that season.

At length the time arrived for obtaining the plates, the Urim and Thummim, and the breastplate. On the twenty-second day of September, one thousand eight hundred and twenty-seven, having gone as usual at the end of another year to the place where they were deposited, the same heavenly messenger delivered them up to me with this charge: that I should be responsible for them; that if I should let them go carelessly, or through any neglect of mine, I should be cut off; but that if I would use all my endeavors to preserve them, until he, the messenger, should call for them, they should be protected.

I soon found out the reason why I had received such strict charges to keep them safe, and why it was that the messenger had said that when I had done what was required at my hand, he would call for them. For no sooner was it known that I had them, than the most strenuous exertions were used to get them from me. Every stratagem that could be invented was resorted to for that purpose. The persecution became more bitter and severe than before, and multitudes were on the alert continually to get them from me if possible. But by the wisdom of God, they remained safe in my hands, until I had accomplished by them what was required at my hand. When, according to arrangements, the messenger called for them, I delivered them up to him; and he has them in his charge until this day, being the second day of May, one thousand eight hundred and thirty-eight.

The excitement, however, still continued, and rumor with her thousand tongues was all the time employed in circulating falsehoods about my father's family, and about myself. If I were to relate a thousandth part of them, it would fill up volumes. The persecution, however, became so intolerable that I was under the necessity of leaving Manchester, and going with my wife to Susquehanna county, in the State of Pennsylvania. While preparing to start—being very poor, and the persecution so heavy upon us that there was no probability that we would ever be otherwise—in the midst of our afflictions we found a friend in a gentleman by the name of Martin Harris, who came to us and gave me fifty dollars to assist us on our journey. Mr. Harris was a resident of Palmyra township, Wayne county, in the State of New York, and a farmer of respectability.

By this timely aid was I enabled to reach the place of my destination in Pennsylvania; and immediately after my arrival there I commenced copying the characters off the plates. I copied a considerable number of them, and by means of the Urim and Thummim I translated some of them, which I did between the time I arrived at the house of my wife's father, in the month of December, and the February following.

Sometime in this month of February, the aforementioned Mr. Martin Harris came to our place, got the characters which I had drawn off the plates, and started with them to the city of

New York. For what took place relative to him and the characters, I refer to his own account of the circumstances, as he related them to me after his return, which was as follows:

"I went to the city of New York, and presented the characters which had been translated, with the translation thereof, to Professor Charles Anthon, a gentleman celebrated for his literary attainments. Professor Anthon stated that the translation was correct, more so than any he had before seen translated from the Egyptian. I then showed him those which were not yet translated, and he said that they were Egyptian, Chaldaic, Assyriac, and Arabic; and he said they were true characters. He gave me a certificate, certifying to the people of Palmyra that they were true characters, and that the translation of such of them as had been translated was also correct. I took the certificate and put it into my pocket, and was just leaving the house, when Mr. Anthon called me back, and asked me how the young man found out that there were gold plates in the place where he found them. I answered that an angel of God had revealed it unto him.

"He then said to me, 'Let me see that certificate.' I accordingly took it out of my pocket and gave it to him, when he took it and tore it to pieces, saying that there was no such thing now as ministering of angels, and that if I would bring the plates to him he would translate them. I informed him that part of the plates were sealed, and that I was forbidden to bring them. He replied, 'I cannot read a sealed book.' I left him and went to Dr. Mitchell, who sanctioned what Professor Anthon had said respecting both the characters and the translation."

On the 5th day of April, 1829, Oliver Cowdery came to my house, until which time I had never seen him. He stated to

116

me that having been teaching school in the neighborhood where my father resided, and my father being one of those who sent to the school, he went to board for a season at his house, and while there the family related to him the circumstances of my having received the plates, and accordingly he had come to make inquiries of me.

Two days after the arrival of Mr. Cowdery (being the 7th of April) I commenced to translate the Book of Mormon, and he began to write for me.

We still continued the work of translation, when, in the ensuing month (May, 1829), we on a certain day went into the woods to pray and inquire of the Lord respecting baptism for the remission of sins, that we found mentioned in the translation of the plates. While we were thus employed, praying and calling upon the Lord, a messenger from heaven descended in a cloud of light, and having laid his hands upon us, he ordained us, saying:

Upon you my fellow servants, in the name of Messiah, I confer the Priesthood of Aaron, which holds the keys of the ministering of angels, and of the gospel of repentance, and of baptism by immersion for the remission of sins; and this shall never be taken again from the earth until the sons of Levi do offer again an offering unto the Lord in righteousness.

He said this Aaronic Priesthood had not the power of laying on hands for the gift of the Holy Ghost, but that this should be conferred on us hereafter; and he commanded us to go and be baptized, and gave us directions that I should baptize Oliver Cowdery, and that afterwards he should baptize me.

Accordingly we went and were baptized. I baptized him first, and afterwards he baptized me—after which I laid my hands upon his head and ordained him to the Aaronic Priesthood, and afterwards he laid his hands on me and ordained me to the same Priesthood—for so we were commanded.

The messenger who visited us on this occasion and conferred this Priesthood upon us, said that his name was John, the same that is called John the Baptist in the New Testament, and that he acted under the direction of Peter, James and John, who held the keys of the Priesthood of Melchizedek, which Priesthood, he said, would in due time be conferred on us, and that I should be called the first Elder of the Church, and he (Oliver Cowdery) the second. It was on the fifteenth day of May, 1829, that we were ordained under the hand of this messenger, and baptized.

Immediately on our coming up out of the water after we had been baptized, we experienced great and glorious blessings from our Heavenly Father. No sooner had I baptized Oliver Cowdery, than the Holy Ghost fell upon him, and he stood up and prophesied many things which should shortly come to pass. And again, so soon as I had been baptized by him, I also had the spirit of prophecy, when, standing up, I prophesied concerning the rise of this Church, and many other things connected with the Church, and this generation of the children of men. We were filled with the Holy Ghost, and rejoiced in the God of our salvation.

Our minds being now enlightened, we began to have the scriptures laid open to our understandings, and the true meaning and intention of their more mysterious passages revealed unto us in a manner which we never could attain to previously, nor ever before had thought of. In the meantime we were forced to keep secret the circumstances of having received the Priesthood and our having been baptized, owing to a spirit of persecution which had already manifested itself in the neighborhood.

We had been threatened with being mobbed, from time to time, and this, too, by professors of religion. And their intentions of mobbing us were only counteracted by the influence of my wife's father's family (under Divine providence), who had become very friendly to me, and who were opposed to mobs, and were willing that I should be allowed to continue the work of translation without interruption; and therefore offered and promised us protection from all unlawful proceedings, as far as in them lay.

A MISSOURI DUNGEON:
...IN PRISONS MORE FREQUENT

Three days after Missouri Governor Boggs signed the Extermination Decree the murdering of Mormons commenced. At Haun's Mill a small settlement of Mormons was overrun by an armed milita-mob. One writer described the conflict as follows: "the facts of 200-250 armed Missourian men attacking thirty (often unarmed) men in the midst of women and children, launching the attack without warning just after a treaty had been agreed, and the lopsided death fatalities (seventeen Mormons, no Missourians) make it a massacre by any definition, not a battle." (*Fire and Sword: A History of the Latter-day Saints in Northern Missouri, 1836-39*, (Salt Lake City: Kofford Books, 2011), p. 319.) Immediately following the massacre, the Missouri Militia established camp a mile south of the city of Far West waiting to lay siege on the Mormons living there. Far West was aware of the slaughter at Haun's Mill, and expected they would be treated likewise.

Joseph Smith was willing to sacrifice his own life, rather than have his followers fight and die. He believed John 15:13 and was willing to act on that belief. On October 31, 1838, a delegation led by George M. Hinckle and including Reed Peck and John Corrill, was sent to negotiate terms for a peaceful resolution. They went to meet the militia under a white flag with instructions to "beg like a dog for peace." Joseph explained that he would "rather go to the State prison himself for twenty years or else die, than have my people exterminated." (John Corrill, *A Brief History of the Church of Jesus Christ of Latter Day Saints Commonly Called Mormons Including an Account of Their Doctrine and Discipline; with the Reasons of the Author for Leaving the Church*, (St. Louis, 1839), pp. 40-41.) The negotiations quickly failed. George Hinckle sent a private message to General Lucas asking to meet alone. Lucas informed Hinckle of four conditions demanded to end the conflict:

1. Give up the Mormon leaders to be tried and punished.

2. To make payment to the Missouri citizens and militia by transferring all their property, and agree to indemnify for all damages done by Mormons.

3. All Mormons must leave Missouri, and would be protected by the militia in their retreat.

4. Mormons must surrender all their arms of any description. (General Lucas Letter to Governor Boggs, November 2, 1838.)

Hinckle accepted the terms. Lucas required compliance with the first term, and demanded the surrender of Joseph Smith, Sidney Rigdon, Lyman Wight, Parley Pratt and George Robinson within the hour. Hinckle returned to Far West, but did not disclose the terms he had accepted. Instead, he reported that General Lucas was willing to meet with Joseph and the other four leaders. They agreed. All five then departed Far West with four of them believing they were to be received as a delegation to discuss resolving the conflict.

Joseph did not intend to surrender on October 31st. When he arrived to negotiate with the commander of the militia, he and his companions were immediately seized and imprisoned. They were disarmed, chained and brought into camp as prisoners. His account recorded, "judge of my surprise, when instead of being treated with that respect which is due from one citizen to another, we were taken as prisoners of war and were treated with the utmost contempt. The officers would not converse with us, and the soldiers, almost to a man, insulted us as much as they felt disposed, breathing out threats against me and my companions." (*DHC* 3:188-189.)

A Missouri Dungeon

The scene that followed was more mob than militia. The chorus of whooping and shrieking in the camp was loud enough to be overheard in Far West. That night the prisoners were chained and guarded in the open air. As rain fell overnight, the prisoners were kept awake by taunting and verbal abuse from their guards. Parley Pratt recorded in his autobiography that the guards mocked, "Come, Mr. Smith, show us an angel." "Give us one of your revelations." "There is one of your brethren here in camp whom we took prisoner yesterday in his own house, and knocked his brains out with his own rifle, which we found hanging over his fireplace; he lays speechless and dying; speak the word and heal him, and then we will all believe." (*Autobiography of Parley P. Pratt*, (Salt Lake City: Deseret Book, 1985), p.160.)

The surrender (or capture) began six months of imprisoned hell for Joseph. It would last until April 16, 1839 when the sheriff who was guarding Joseph allowed him and fellow prisoners to escape. They fled Missouri and arrived in Illinois on April 22, 1839.

Following the first miserable night of capture, things worsened. On November 1, 1838, the following order was issued by the commanding general of the Missouri State Militia: "To Brigadier-General Doniphan: Sir: You will take Joseph Smith and the other prisoners into the public square of Far West and shoot them at 9:00 tomorrow morning. Samuel D. Lucas, Major-General Commanding." To the order Doniphan responded: "It is cold-blooded murder. I will not obey your order. My brigade shall march for Liberty tomorrow morning, at 8 o'clock; and if you execute these men, I will hold you responsible before an earthly tribunal, so help me God. A. W. Doniphan, Brigadier-General." (*History of Caldwell and Livingston Counties Missouri*, (St. Louis: National Historical Co., 1886), p. 137.)

A Man Without Doubt

Although he disobeyed a direct order from his commanding officer, no disciplinary action was taken against General Doniphan. General Lucas' attention immediately turned to the Mormons left in Far West. The day after Joseph's arrest, Far West surrendered. After Far West had been subdued, the militia-mob rode into town, ransacked houses, arrested people, including Joseph's brother Hyrum Smith, and specifically targeted Joseph's family for abuse. Emma Smith and her children were driven out of their home, everything was stolen, and the family mistreated.

The men guarding the prisoners grew bolder in their insults after the sacking of Far West. They added tales of the sexual abuse and rape of women. This was a claim the prisoners were in no position to doubt. Atop all the other uncertainties, Joseph had to wonder about his wife and the safety of his family. Emma Smith was targeted by the mob, but how much abuse she took is not certain. There were women in Far West who had been raped. (*DHC*, Vol. 3, p. XVII.) Approximately four years later Emma Smith was living in Illinois. She corresponded with Governor Thomas Carlin about the abuse they endured in Missouri. Her letter does not provide details of what she and her children suffered, but confirmed there had been "many cruel and illegal operations of Lilburn W. Boggs, and the consequent suffering of myself and family[.]" She confirmed that her "heart burned with just indignation, towards our calumniators, as well as the perpetrators of those horrid crimes." She did not write down the details, but she characterized them as "afflictions and many sufferings which cannot be uttered[.]" (*JS Papers, Journals Vol. 2*, pp. 112-113, letter of Emma Smith to Thomas Carlin, August 16, 1842.)

The sexual assault of Mormon women would not have been widely admitted by the victims. A 2016 historical conference sponsored by Brigham Young University included a talk discussing the gang-rape of a prominent Mormon woman named Eliza R. Snow, who would later become the president of the LDS church's women's organization. The talk relied on the oral transmission of an account through a grandmother, later written into journal many years after the victim's death. An article based on the talk, *Eliza R. Snow as a Victim of Sexual Violence in the 1838 Missouri War– the Author's Reflections on a Source*, was published in the March 7, 2016 in the Juvenile Instructor, Andrea Radke-Moss, (www. Juvenile instructor.org).

Joseph Smith also mentioned the abuse suffered in Missouri in a letter written in 1842 to the editor of the Chicago Democrat, John Wentworth, which he subsequently republished in the Mormon newspaper *Times and Seasons*. In his letter he confirmed that at the hands of the Missouri mobs "the chastity of our women was violated." (*Times and Seasons*, Vol. III, No. 9, March 1, 1842, "Church History.")

There could be no better way for the mob to discourage Joseph Smith and those he led from returning to Missouri to build a city of Zion than to abuse him, his wife and children. They wanted to turn Joseph's vision of a city of peace and place of safety into memories of horror, helplessness and hopelessness. If they did not succeed in killing him, they wanted to forever repel him.

The day after the raid on Far West, the prisoners were taken back to town in chains. The guards allowed Joseph to enter his ransacked house to briefly visit with his family. Emma broke down in tears, his children were panicked, and his young son asked if the mob was going to kill his father. A guard responded that this would be the last time the family would see Joseph alive. Joseph's elderly mother was likewise taunted by the guards and told that her sons (Joseph and Hyrum) "would never return alive." (Lucy Mack Smith, *History of Joseph Smith, the Prophet, by His Mother,* (Salt Lake City: Bookcraft), p. 290.)

Based on the terms of the "surrender" negotiated the day before, the residents of Far West were informed they were to transfer their property to the Missourians, leave the state, and never return. A table was set up in the town square and the Mormons filed to the table at gunpoint to sign a document conveying all their real estate and personal property to make "reparations" for the costs Missouri incurred in the conflict. John Corrill estimated 500 men signed away all their property.

Under the guard of General Moses Wilson, the prisoners were marched toward Independence. Wilson seemed protective of the prisoners and, according to Pratt, informed them on the first day of the march, "I'll be damn'd if anybody shall hurt you. We just intend to exhibit you in Independence, let the people look at you and see what a damn'd set of fine fellows you are. And, more particularly, to keep you from that G-d damn'd old bigot of a Gen. Clark and his troops, from down country, who are so stuffed full of lies and prejudice that they would shoot you down in a moment." (Pratt, *Autobiography*, pp. 163-164.) The next morning Joseph prophesied to his fellow-prisoners that none of them would be killed in the coming ordeal, which turned out to be true.

Along the route to Independence, General Wilson often stopped to display the prisoners. He would refer to each of the captives by name. This spectacle continued throughout the route, and although they arrived at Independence in a downpour, a crowd of hundreds gathered to see the infamous captives. Pratt said it "served the same purpose that a caravan of wild animals would for a show." (Pratt, *Times and Seasons*, Vol. 1, (September, 1840), p. 161.)

At Independence, General Wilson entertained Joseph at his own home part of the time and is reported to have later said, "He was a remarkable man. I carried him into my house a prisoner in chains, and in less than two hours my wife loved him better than she did me." (Donna Hill, *Joseph Smith: The First Mormon*, (New York: Doubleday, 1977), pp. 245-246.) Wilson's benign custody was short lived, and the prisoners were soon returned to the possession of abusive guards.

The abuse Joseph and his fellow prisoners endured was motivated by the public agitation before and after hostilities erupted, the charge of treason, and the conviction that the prisoners deserved to die. They were viewed as a threat to peace and order. The guards thought they deserved punishment, and abusing them was a natural extension of the prevailing circumstances.

Colonel Sterling Price took the prisoners to Richmond, Missouri for a preliminary hearing on criminal charges. Because there were threats that the prisoners would be killed while enroute, Price rode ahead to Richmond on the last day of the trip and returned with 100 troops to guard the final leg of the journey.

The verbal abuse of the prisoners renewed in Richmond. Fellow prisoner Pratt recorded an incident one night while confined in Richmond:

> In one of those tedious nights we had lain as if in sleep till the hour of midnight had passed, and our ears and hearts had been pained, while we had listened for hours to the obscene jests, the horrid oaths, the dreadful blasphemies and filthy language of our guards, Colonel Price at their head, as they recounted to each other their deeds of rapine, murder, robbery, etc., which they had committed among the 'Mormons' while at Far West and vicinity. They even boasted of defiling by force wives, daughters and virgins, and of shooting or dashing out the brains of men, women and children.

A Man Without Doubt

I had listened till I became so disgusted, shocked, horrified, and so filled with the spirit of indignant justice that I could scarcely refrain from rising upon my feet and rebuking the guards; but had said nothing to Joseph, or any one else, although I lay next to him and knew he was awake. On a sudden he arose to his feet, and spoke in a voice of thunder, or as the roaring lion, uttering, as near as I can recollect, the following words:

"SILENCE, ye fiends of the infernal pit. In the name of Jesus Christ I rebuke you, and command you to be still; I will not live another minute and hear such language. Cease such talk, or you or I die THIS INSTANT!"

He ceased to speak. He stood erect in terrible majesty. Chained, and without a weapon; calm, unruffled and dignified as an angel, he looked upon the quailing guards, whose weapons were lowered or dropped to the ground; whose knees smote together, and who, shrinking into a corner or crouching at his feet, begged his pardon, and remained quiet till a change of guards.

I have seen the ministers of justice, clothed in magisterial robes, and criminals arraigned before them, while life was suspended on a breath, in the Courts of England; I have witnessed a Congress in solemn session to give laws to nations; I have tried to conceive of kings of royal courts, of thrones and crowns; and of emperors assembled to decide the fate of kingdoms; but dignity and majesty have I seen but once, as it stood in chains, at midnight, in a dungeon in an obscure village of

A Missouri Dungeon

Missouri. (*Autobiography of Parley P. Pratt*, supra, pp. 179-180.)

There was a disagreement between General Clark and Governor Boggs over the correct course to take. Clark believed the legal dispute involved misconduct at a time of war, and therefore the men could be tried before a general military court. The Governor thought a civilian court was required. Clark asked the state's Attorney General to decide the question. Ultimately a hearing was conducted before the civilian court of Circuit Judge Austin A. King. They were charged with murder, burglary, arson, robbery, larceny, and high treason against the State of Missouri. The hearing lasted from November 12 to 28.

While at Richmond, the prisoners were chained together to prevent escape. They remained in chains from November 10 to November 29. At the hearing, three of the five Mormon negotiators at Far West, Hinckle, Peck and Corrill, testified against the prisoners. All three left the Mormon faith as a result.

During the hearing, in addition to the other Mormon witnesses who testifed against the prisoners, Sampson Avard provided the most damning evidence. Sampson Avard led the underground Danites, but testified their society was authorized, organized and supervised by Joseph Smith, who he claimed also participated in their acts. He identified Joseph with raids against Missouri farms and settlements, where Danites pillaged and destroyed. Although Avard did not claim to have been present during some of these events, he claimed to have seen Joseph returning with others under his command transporting stock animals and other spoils stolen from Missourians.

Avard testified that Joseph expected participants to swear binding oaths to the effect that they would be put to death if they revealed Danite secrets. The testimony, if it were true, would have put Avard's life in jeopardy by revealing the band's secrets. Nothing of the sort happened. There was no retaliation by Joseph or any Mormon. Following his testimony against Joseph Smith, Avard lived peaceably in Illinois until his death in 1869, unmolested by those he betrayed.

Avard was the first and chief witness in the hearing. Joseph claimed that he learned of Avard's Danite activities for the first time as he testified in the Missouri courtroom. Unfortunately, he also learned that he was the claimed author, inspiration and director of the Danite violence. The general who was in charge of the Missouri militia wrote to Governor Boggs and said that he did not believe he could have convicted any of the Mormon leaders if Avard had not provided testimony against them. (Report of General Clark, November 29, 1838.)

In all, 42 witnesses were called. The most damning testimony always came from former, disaffected Mormons. They uniformly testified they withdrew from the Mormon church because of the church leaders' ambition to build a kingdom that would break all other governments into pieces. They said Mormon ambition was based on the Book of Daniel Chapter 2:44 and 7:9,18, 22 and 27. Belief in *Bible* prophecy was enough to prove "treason" against Missouri. There was no defense permitted in the preliminary hearing, and therefore none was presented. The purpose was only to determine if the prisoners would stand trial for crimes. The court decided that 11 would be tried. On the charge of treason, 6 men would face trial: Joseph Smith, Hyrum Smith, Sidney Rigdon, Lyman Wight, Caleb Baldwin and Alexander McRay. These 6 were separated from the other prisoners and sent to the Clay County prison. On the charge of murder, 5 men were held: Morris Phelps, Luman Gibbs, Darwin Chase, Norman Shearer, and Parley Pratt. They would remain in Richmond.

A Missouri Dungeon

The six charged with treason were transported on November 29, 1839 to Liberty Jail. Judge King's order directed the jailor in Liberty to hold the prisoners in "custody in the jail of the said county of Clay, there to remain until they be delivered therefrom by due course of law." (Austin A. King, District Court Judge, November 29, 1838.)

The first released was Sidney Rigdon in January 1839. Fearing for his safety he remained in prison until February, then departed Missouri for the last time.

The Liberty Jail was small. It was built with double walls. The outer wall was thick rock and inner rough-hewn oak. The walls of the small prison were four feet thick. There were two levels, an upper floor with a ceiling that was over 7 feet high, and a lower dungeon with a ceiling height not quite 6 feet. In the dungeon there were two windows, one on the north and one on the south. The windows were 2 feet long and 6 inches wide with a single iron bar running the two-foot length. The room was approximately 14 feet by 14 feet. The windows had no glass, and winter conditions were cold and dismal.

The prisoners suffered from the cold, poor hygiene, poor food quality, and verbal abuse by the guards. All those held in Liberty reported that on multiple occasions they were fed food that had been poisoned. The guards told their prisoners they were serving them flesh from a deceased black slave. Whether this was true or not, all but one of the prisoners refused to eat for five days. The guards called this purported dead slave flesh "Mormon beef." Lyman Wight, who was the only one to eat it, wrote, "from extreme hunger, I was compelled to eat it." (Lyman Wight, Testimony, *DHC*, Vol. 3:448.) The prisoners reported that their food was filthy, and they would only eat when potential starvation compelled it. The bitterest reflection for Joseph was that the calamity fell upon them because of the betrayal of "Mormon dissenters." In one of his letters he named the dissidents responsible:

Hinkle, Corrill, Phelps, Avard, Reed Peck, Cleminson, McLellin, John Whitmer, O. Cowdery, Martin Harris, Marsh, and Hyde. These had been prominent leaders, trusted friends, and one-time believers in Mormonism. It was false testimony by those from within the flock that led to imprisonment of the leaders.

Occasional letters from friends and family lifted the spirits of the prisoners. In response to one letter Joseph received, he wrote what comprises the next chapter. It was written after 5 months (145 days) of imprisonment and suffering. At the time he was writing this letter, he had no idea when or how the ordeal would end. The letter was composed under the most trying of circumstances, but does not reflect the mistreatment underway. It is a rare thing for an American prisoner to believe he is called upon to suffer for the sake of his belief in Christ. The alignment of circumstances provided Joseph Smith with a unique opportunity to show what was in his heart.

The letter in the next chapter belongs alongside other Christian statements of faith, hope and charity. He leaves vengeance to God. It provides a look into Joseph Smith's heart and mind. In it there can be found no doubting God, no uncertainty about the course he was on, no doubt about the ultimate outcome remaining in God's hands.

Three short excerpts from this letter have been canonized by the LDS church in their *Doctrine and Covenants*. They are *D&C* Sections 121, 122 and 123.

The month after he wrote this letter, in April 1839 the remaining 5 prisoners were allowed to escape. Missouri authorities concluded it would be better to have them fugitives and escapees than acquitted and innocent.

JOSEPH'S LETTER FROM LIBERTY: ...IN PERILS BY MY OWN COUNTRYMEN

LIBERTY JAIL, CLAY COUNTY, MISSOURI, March 25, 1839.

To the Church of Latter-day Saints at Quincy, Illinois, and Scattered Abroad, and to Bishop Partridge in Particular:

Your humble servant, Joseph Smith, Jun., prisoner for the Lord Jesus Christ's sake, and for the Saints, taken and held by the power of mobocracy, under the exterminating reign of his excellency, the governor, Lilburn W. Boggs, in company with his fellow prisoners and beloved brethren, Caleb Baldwin, Lyman Wight, Hyrum Smith, and Alexander McRae, send unto you all greeting. May the grace of God the Father, and of our Lord and Savior Jesus Christ, rest upon you all, and abide with you forever. May knowledge be multiplied unto you by the mercy of God. And may faith and virtue, and knowledge and temperance, and patience and godliness, and brotherly kindness and charity be in you and abound, that you may not be barren in anything, nor unfruitful.

For inasmuch as we know that the most of you are well acquainted with the wrongs and the high-handed injustice and cruelty that are practiced upon us; whereas we have been taken prisoners charged falsely with every kind of evil, and thrown into prison, enclosed with strong walls, surrounded with a strong guard, who continually watch day and night as indefatigable as the devil does in tempting and laying snares for the people of God:

Therefore, dearly beloved brethren, we are the more ready and willing to lay claim to your fellowship and love. For our circumstances are calculated to awaken our spirits to a sacred remembrance of everything, and we think that yours are also, and that nothing therefore can separate us from the

133

love of God and fellowship one with another; and that every species of wickedness and cruelty practiced upon us will only tend to bind our hearts together and seal them together in love. We have no need to say to you that we are held in bonds without cause, neither is it needful that you say unto us, We are driven from our homes and smitten without cause. We mutually understand that if the inhabitants of the state of Missouri had let the Saints alone, and had been as desirable of peace as they were, there would have been nothing but peace and quietude in the state unto this day; we should not have been in this hell, surrounded with demons (if not those who are damned, they are those who shall be damned) and where we are compelled to hear nothing but blasphemous oaths, and witness a scene of blasphemy, and drunkenness and hypocrisy, and debaucheries of every description.

And again, the cries of orphans and widows would not have ascended up to God against them. Nor would innocent blood have stained the soil of Missouri. But oh! the unrelenting hand! The inhumanity and murderous disposition of this people! It shocks all nature; it beggars and defies all description; it is a tale of woe; a lamentable tale; yea a sorrowful tale; too much to tell; too much for contemplation; too much for human beings; it cannot be found among the heathens; it cannot be found among the nations where kings and tyrants are enthroned; it cannot be found among the savages of the wilderness; yea, and I think it cannot be found among the wild and ferocious beasts of the forest-- that a man should be mangled for sport! Women be robbed of all that they have--their last morsel for subsistence, and then be violated to gratify the hellish desires of the mob, and finally left to perish with their helpless offspring clinging around their necks.

But this is not all. After a man is dead, he must be dug up from his grave and mangled to pieces, for no other purpose than to gratify their spleen against the religion of God.

They practice these things upon the Saints, who have done them no wrong, who are innocent and virtuous; who loved the Lord their God, and were willing to forsake all things for Christ's sake. These things are awful to relate, but they are verily true. It must needs be that offenses come, but woe unto them by whom they come.

Oh God! where art Thou? And where is the pavilion that covereth Thy hiding place? How long shall Thy hand be stayed, and Thine eye, yea Thy pure eye, behold from the eternal heavens, the wrongs of Thy people, and of Thy servants, and Thy ear be penetrated with their cries? Yea, O Lord, how long shall they suffer these wrongs and unlawful oppressions, before Thine heart shall be softened towards them, and Thy bowels be moved with compassion towards them?

O Lord God Almighty, Maker of Heaven, Earth and Seas, and of all things that in them are, and who controllest and subjectest the devil, and the dark and benighted dominion of Sheol! Stretch forth Thy hand, let Thine eye pierce; let Thy pavilion be taken up; let Thy hiding place no longer be covered; let Thine ear be inclined; let Thine heart be softened, and Thy bowels moved with compassion towards us, Let Thine anger be kindled against our enemies; and in the fury of Thine heart, with Thy sword avenge us of our wrongs; remember Thy suffering Saints, O our God! and Thy servants will rejoice in Thy name forever.

Dearly and beloved brethren, we see that perilous times have come, as was testified of. We may look, then, with most perfect assurance, for the fulfillment of all those things that have been written, and with more confidence than ever before, lift up our eyes to the luminary of day, and say in our hearts, Soon thou wilt veil thy blushing face. He that said "Let there be light," and there was light, hath spoken this word. And again, Thou moon, thou dimmer light, thou luminary of night, shalt turn to blood.

We see that everything is being fulfilled; and that the time shall soon come when the Son of Man shall descend in the clouds of heaven. Our hearts do not shrink, neither are our spirits altogether broken by the grievous yoke which is put upon us. We know that God will have our oppressors in derision; that He will laugh at their calamity, and mock when their fear cometh.

O that we could be with you, brethren, and unbosom our feelings to you! We would tell, that we should have been liberated at the time Elder Rigdon was, on the writ of habeas corpus, had not our own lawyers interpreted the law, contrary to what it reads, against us; which prevented us from introducing our evidence before the mock court.

They have done us much harm from the beginning. They have of late acknowledged that the law was misconstrued, and tantalized our feelings with it, and have entirely forsaken us, and have forfeited their oaths and their bonds; and we have a come-back on them, for they are co-workers with the mob.

As nigh as we can learn, the public mind has been for a long time turning in our favor, and the majority is now friendly; and the lawyers can no longer browbeat us by saying that this or that is a matter of public opinion, for public opinion is not willing to brook it; for it is beginning to look with feelings of indignation against our oppressors, and to say that the "Mormons" were not in the fault in the least. We think that truth, honor, virtue and innocence will eventually come out triumphant. We should have taken a habeas corpus before the high judge and escaped the mob in a summary way; but unfortunately for us, the timber of the wall being very hard, our auger handles gave out, and hindered us longer than we expected; we applied to a friend, and a very slight incautious act gave rise to some suspicions, and before we could fully succeed, our plan was discovered; we had everything in readiness, but the last stone, and we could have made our escape in one minute, and should have succeeded admirably, had it not been for a little imprudence or over-anxiety on the part of our friend.

The sheriff and jailer did not blame us for our attempt; it was a fine breach, and cost the county a round sum; but public opinion says that we ought to have been permitted to have made our escape; that then the disgrace would have been on us, but now it must come on the state; that there cannot be any charge sustained against us; and that the conduct of the mob, the murders committed at Haun's Mills, and the exterminating order of the governor, and the one-sided, rascally proceedings of the legislature, have damned the state of Missouri to all eternity. I would just name also that General Atchison has proved himself as contemptible as any of them.

We have tried for a long time to get our lawyers to draw us some petitions to the supreme judges of this state. But they utterly refused. We have examined the law, and drawn the petitions ourselves, and have obtained abundance of proof to counteract all the testimony that was against us, so that if the supreme judge does not grant us our liberty, he has to act without cause, contrary to honor, evidence, law or justice, sheerly to please the devil, but we hope better things and trust before many days God will so order our case, that we shall be set at liberty and take up our habitation with the Saints.

We received some letters last evening--one from Emma, one from Don C. Smith, and one from Bishop Partridge--all breathing a kind and consoling spirit. We were much gratified with their contents. We had been a long time without information; and when we read those letters they were to our souls as the gentle air is refreshing, but our joy was mingled with grief, because of the sufferings of the poor and much injured Saints. And we need not say to you that the floodgates of our hearts were lifted and our eyes were a fountain of tears, but those who have not been enclosed in the walls of prison without cause or provocation, can have but little idea how sweet the voice of a friend is; one token of friendship from any source whatever awakens and calls into action every sympathetic feeling; it brings up in an instant everything that is passed; it seizes the present with the avidity of lightning; it grasps after the future with the fierceness of a tiger; it moves the mind backward and forward, from one thing to another, until finally all enmity, malice and hatred, and past differences, misunderstandings and mismanagements are slain victorious at the feet of hope; and when the heart is sufficiently contrite, then the voice of inspiration steals along and whispers, My son, peace be unto thy soul; thine adversity and thine afflictions shall be but a small moment; and then if thou endure it well, God shall exalt thee on high; thou shalt triumph over all thy foes; thy friends do stand by thee, and they shall hail thee again, with warm hearts and friendly hands; thou art not yet as Job; thy friends do not contend against thee, neither charge thee with transgression, as they did Job; and they who do charge thee with transgression, their hope shall be blasted and their prospects shall melt away as the hoar frost melteth before the burning rays of the rising sun; and also that God hath set His hand and Seal to change the times and seasons, and to blind their minds, that they may not understand His marvelous workings, that He may prove them also and take them in their own craftiness; also because their hearts are corrupted, and the things which they are willing to bring upon others, and love to have others suffer, may come upon themselves to the very uttermost; that they may be disappointed also, and their hopes may be cut off; and not many years hence, that they and their posterity shall be

138

swept from under heaven, saith God, that not one of them is left to stand by the wall. Cursed are all those that shall lift up the heel against mine anointed. saith the Lord, and cry they have sinned when they have not sinned before me, saith the Lord, but have done that which was meet in mine eyes, and which I commanded them; but those who cry transgression do it because they are the servants of sin and are the children of disobedience themselves; and those who swear falsely against my servants, that they might bring them into bondage and death; wo unto them; because they have offended my little ones; they shall be severed from the ordinances of mine house; their basket shall not be full, and their houses and their barns shall perish, and they themselves shall be despised by those that flattered them; they shall not have right to the Priesthood, nor their posterity after them, from generation to generation; it had been better for them that a millstone had been hanged about their necks, and they drowned in the depth of the sea.

Wo unto all those that discomfort my people, and drive and murder, and testify against them, saith the Lord of Hosts; a generation of vipers shall not escape the damnation of hell. Behold mine eyes see and know all their works, and I have in reserve a swift judgment in the season thereof, for them all; for there is a time appointed for every man according as his work shall be.

And now, beloved brethren, we say unto you, that inasmuch as God hath said that He would have a tried people, that He would purge them as gold, now we think that this time He has chosen His own crucible, wherein we have been tried; and we think if we get through with any degree of safety, and shall have kept the faith, that it will be a sign to this generation, altogether sufficient to leave them without excuse; and we think also, it will be a trial of our faith equal to that of Abraham, and that the ancients will not have whereof to boast over us in the day of judgment, as being called to pass through heavier afflictions; that we may hold an even weight in the balance with them; but now, after having suffered so great sacrifice and having passed through so great a season of sorrow, we trust that a ram may be caught in the thicket speedily, to relieve the sons and daughters of Abraham from their great anxiety, and to light up the lamp of salvation upon their countenances, that they may hold on now, after having gone so far unto everlasting life.

Now, brethren, concerning the places for the location of the Saints we cannot counsel you as we could if we were present with you; and as to the things that were written heretofore, we did not consider them anything very binding, therefore we now say once for all, that we think it most proper that the general affairs of the Church, which are necessary to be considered, while your humble servant remains in bondage, should be transacted by a general conference of the most faithful and the most respectable of the authorities of the Church, and a minute of those transactions may be kept, and forwarded from time to time, to your humble servant; and if there should be any corrections by the word of the Lord, they shall be freely transmitted, and your humble servant will approve all things whatsoever is acceptable unto God. If anything should have been suggested by us, or any names mentioned, except by commandment, or thus saith the Lord, we do not consider it binding; therefore our hearts shall not be grieved if different arrangements should be entered into. Nevertheless we would suggest the propriety of being aware of an aspiring spirit, which spirit has often times urged men forward to make foul speeches, and influence the Church to reject milder counsels, and has eventually been the means of bringing much death and sorrow upon the Church.

We would say, beware of pride also; for well and truly hath the wise man said, that pride goeth before destruction, and a haughty spirit before a fall. And again, outward appearance is not always a criterion by which to judge our fellow man; but the lips betray the haughty and overbearing imaginations of the heart; by his words and his deeds let him be judged. Flattery also is a deadly poison. A frank and open rebuke provoketh a good man to emulation; and in the hour of trouble he will be your best friend; but on the other hand, it will draw out all the corruptions of corrupt hearts, and lying and the poison of asps is under their tongues; and they do cause the pure in heart to be cast into prison, because they want them out of their way.

A fanciful and flowery and heated imagination beware of; because the things of God are of deep import; and time, and experience, and careful and ponderous and solemn thoughts can only find them out. Thy mind, O man, if thou wilt lead a soul unto salvation, must stretch as high as the utmost heavens, and search into and contemplate the darkest abyss, and the broad expanse of eternity--thou must commune with God. How much more dignified and noble are the thoughts of God, than the vain imaginations of the human heart! None but fools will trifle with the souls of men.

How vain and trifling have been our spirits, our conferences, our councils, our meetings, our private as well as public conversations--too low, too mean, too vulgar, too condescending for the dignified characters of the called and chosen of God, according to the purposes of His will, from before the foundation of the world! We are called to hold the keys of the mysteries of those things that have been kept hid from the foundation of the world until now. Some have tasted a little of these things, many of which are to be poured down from heaven upon the heads of babes; yea, upon the weak, obscure and despised ones of the earth. Therefore we beseech of you, brethren, that you bear with those who do not feel themselves more worthy than yourselves, while we exhort one another to a reformation with one and all, both old and young, teachers and taught, both high and low, rich and poor, bond and free, male and female; let honesty, and sobriety, and candor, and solemnity, and virtue, and pureness, and meekness, and simplicity crown our heads in every place; and in fine, become as little children, without malice, guile or hypocrisy.

And now, brethren, after your tribulations, if you do these things, and exercise fervent prayer and faith in the sight of God always, He shall give unto you knowledge by His Holy Spirit, yea by the unspeakable gift of the Holy Ghost, that has not been revealed since the world was until now; which our forefathers have waited with anxious expectation to be revealed in the last times, which their minds were pointed to by the angels, as held in reserve for the fullness of their glory; a time to come in the which nothing shall be withheld. whether there be one God or many Gods, they shall be manifest; all thrones and dominions, principalities and powers, shall be revealed and set forth upon all who have endured valiantly for the Gospel of Jesus Christ; and also if there be bounds set to the heavens, or to the seas; or to the dry land, or to the sun, moon or stars; all the times of their revolutions; all the appointed days, months and years, and all the days of their days, months and years, and all their glories, laws, and set times, shall be revealed, in the days of the dispensation of the fullness of times, according to that which was ordained in the midst of the Council of the Eternal God of all other Gods, before this world was, that should be reserved unto the finishing and the end thereof, when every man shall enter into His eternal presence, and into His immortal rest.

But I beg leave to say unto you, brethren, that ignorance, superstition and bigotry placing itself where it ought not, is oftentimes in the way of the prosperity of this Church; like the torrent of rain from the mountains, that floods the most pure and crystal stream with mire, and dirt, and filthiness, and obscures everything that was clear before, and all rushes along in one general deluge; but time weathers tide; and notwithstanding we are rolled in the mire of the flood for the time being, the next surge peradventure, as time rolls on, may bring to us the fountain as clear as crystal, and as pure as snow; while the filthiness, floodwood and rubbish is left and purged out by the way.

How long can rolling water remain impure? What power shall stay the heavens? As well might man stretch forth his puny arm to stop the Missouri river in its decreed course, or to turn it up stream, as to hinder the Almighty from pouring down knowledge from heaven, upon the heads of the Latter-day Saints.

What is Boggs or his murderous party, but wimbling willows upon the shore to catch the flood-wood? As well might we argue that water is not water, because the mountain torrents send down mire and roil the crystal stream, although afterwards render it more pure than before; or that fire is not fire, because it is of a quenchable nature, by pouring on the flood; as to say that our cause is down because renegades, liars, priests, thieves and murderers, who are all alike tenacious of their crafts and creeds, have poured down, from their spiritual wickedness in high places, and from their strongholds of the devil, a flood of dirt and mire and filthiness and vomit upon our heads.

No! God forbid. Hell may pour forth its rage like the burning lava of mount Vesuvius, or of Etna, or of the most terrible of the burning mountains; and yet shall "Mormonism" stand. Water, fire, truth and God are all realities. Truth is "Mormonism." God is the author of it. He is our shield. It is by Him we received our birth. It was by His voice that we were called to a dispensation of His Gospel in the beginning of the fullness of times. It was by Him we received the Book of Mormon; and it is by Him that we remain unto this day; and by Him we shall remain, if it shall be for our glory; and in His Almighty name we are determined to endure tribulation as good soldiers unto the end.

But, brethren, we shall continue to offer further reflections in our next epistle. You will learn by the time you have read this, and if you do not learn it, you may learn it, that walls and irons, doors and creaking hinges, and half-scared-to-death guards and jailers, grinning like some damned spirits, lest an innocent man should make his escape to bring to light the damnable deeds of a murderous mob, are calculated in their very nature to make the soul of an honest man feel stronger than the powers of hell.

But we must bring our epistle to a close. We send our respects to fathers, mothers, wives and children, brothers and sisters; we hold them in the most sacred remembrance.

We feel to inquire after Elder Rigdon; if he has not forgotten us, it has not been signified to us by his writing. Brother George W. Robinson also; and Elder Cahoon, we remember him, but would like to jog his memory a little on the fable of the bear and the two friends who mutually agreed to stand by each other. And perhaps it would not be amiss to mention uncle John [Smith], and various others. A word of consolation and a blessing would not come amiss from anybody, while we are being so closely whispered by the bear. But we feel to excuse everybody and everything, yea the more readily when we contemplate that we are in the hands of persons worse that a bear, for the bear would not prey upon a dead carcass.

Letter from Liberty Jail

Our respects and love and fellowship to all the virtuous Saints. We are your brethren and fellow-sufferers, and prisoners of Jesus Christ for the Gospel's sake, and for the hope of glory which is in us. Amen.

We continue to offer further reflections to Bishop Partridge, and to the Church of Jesus Christ of Latter-day Saints, whom we love with a fervent love, and do always bear them in mind in all our prayers to the throne of God.

It still seems to bear heavily on our minds that the Church would do well to secure to themselves the contract of the land which is proposed to them by Mr. Isaac Galland, and to cultivate the friendly feelings of that gentleman, inasmuch as he shall prove himself to be a man of honor and a friend to humanity; also Isaac Van Allen, Esq., the attorney-general of Iowa Territory, and Governor Lucas, that peradventure such men may be wrought upon by the providence of God, to do good unto His people. We really think that Mr. Galland's letter breathes that kind of a spirit, if we may judge correctly. Governor Lucas also. We suggest the idea of praying fervently for all men who manifest any degree of sympathy for the suffering children of God.

We think that the United States Surveyor of the Iowa Territory may be of great benefit to the Church, if it be the will of God to this end; and righteousness should be manifested as the girdle of our loins.

It seems to be deeply impressed upon our minds that the Saints ought to lay hold of every door that shall seem to be opened unto them, to obtain foothold on the earth, and be making all the preparation that is within their power for the terrible storms that are now gathering in the heavens, "a day of clouds, with darkness and gloominess, and of thick darkness," as spoken of by the Prophets, which cannot be now of a long time lingering, for there seems to be a whispering that the angels of heaven who have been entrusted with the counsel of these matters for the last days, have taken counsel together; and among the rest of the general affairs that have to be transacted in their honorable council, they have taken cognizance of the testimony of those who were murdered at Hauns Mills, and also those who were martyred with David W. Patten. and elsewhere, and have passed some decisions peradventure in favor of the Saints, and those who were called to suffer without cause.

These decisions will be made known in their time; and the council will take into consideration all those things that offend.

We have a fervent desire that in your general conferences everything should be discussed with a great deal of care and propriety, lest you grieve the Holy Spirit, which shall be poured out at all times upon your heads, when you are exercised with those principles of righteousness that are agreeable to the mind of God, and are properly affected one toward another, and are careful by all means to remember, those who are in bondage, and in heaviness, and in deep affliction for your sakes. And if there are any among you who aspire after their own aggrandizement, and seek their own opulence, while their brethren are groaning in poverty, and are under sore trials and temptations, they cannot be benefited by the intercession of the Holy Spirit, which maketh intercession for us day and night with groanings that cannot be uttered.

We ought at all times to be very careful that such high-mindedness shall never have place in our hearts; but condescend to men of low estate, and with all long-suffering bear the infirmities of the weak.

Behold, there are many called, but few are chosen. And why are they not chosen? Because their hearts are set so much upon the things of this world, and aspire to the honors of men, that they do not learn this one lesson--that the rights of the Priesthood are inseparably connected with the powers of heaven, and that the powers of heaven cannot be controlled nor handed only upon the principles of righteousness. That they may be conferred upon us, it is true; but when we undertake to cover our sins, or to gratify our pride, our vain ambition, or to exorcise control, or dominion, or compulsion, upon the souls of the children of men, in any degree of unrighteousness, behold, the heavens withdraw themselves; the Spirit of the Lord is grieved; and when it is withdrawn, Amen to the Priesthood, or the authority of that men. Behold! ere he is aware, he is left unto himself, to kick against the pricks; to persecute the Saints, and to fight against God.

We have learned by sad experience that it is the nature and disposition of almost all men, as soon as they get a little authority, as they suppose, they will immediately begin to exercise unrighteous dominion. Hence many are called, but few are chosen.

No power or influence can or ought to be maintained by virtue of the Priesthood, only by persuasion, by long-suffering, by gentleness, and meekness, and by love unfeigned; by kindness, and pure knowledge, which shall greatly enlarge the soul without hypocrisy, and without guile, reproving betimes with sharpness, when moved upon by the Holy Ghost, and then showing forth afterwards an increase of love toward him whom thou hast reproved, lest he esteem thee to be his enemy; that he may know that thy faithfulness is stronger than the cords of death; let thy bowels also be full of charity towards all men, and to the household of faith, and let virtue garnish thy thoughts unceasingly, then shall thy confidence wax strong in the presence of God, and the doctrine of the Priesthood shall distill upon thy soul as the dews from heaven. The Holy Ghost shall be thy constant companion, and thy sceptre an unchanging sceptre of righteousness and truth, and thy dominion shall be an everlasting dominion, and without compulsory means it shall flow unto thee forever and ever.

The ends of the earth shall inquire after thy name, and fools shall have thee in derision, and hell shall rage against thee, while the pure in heart, and the wise, and the noble, and the virtuous, shall seek counsel, and authority and blessing constantly from under thy hand, and thy people shall never be turned against thee by the testimony of traitors; and although their influence shall cast thee into trouble, and into bars and walls, thou shalt be had in honor, and but for a small moment and thy voice shall be more terrible in the midst of thine enemies, than the fierce lion, because of thy righteousness; and thy God shall stand by thee forever and ever.

If thou art called to pass through tribulations; if thou art in perils among false brethren; if thou art in perils among robbers; if thou art in perils by land or by sea; if thou art accused with all manner of false accusations if thine enemies fall upon thee; if they tear thee from the society of thy father and mother and brethren and sisters, and if with a drawn sword thine enemies tear thee from the bosom of thy wife, and of thine offspring, and thine elder son, although but six years of age, shall cling to thy garment, and shall say, My father, my father, why can't you stay with us? O, my father, what are the men going to do with you? and if then he shall be thrust from thee by the sword, and thou be dragged to prison, and thine enemies prowl around thee like wolves for the blood of the lamb; and if thou should be cast into the pit, or into the hands of murderers, and the sentence of death passed upon thee; if thou be cast into the deep; if the billowing surge conspire against thee; if fierce winds become thine enemy; if the heavens gather blackness, and all the elements combine to hedge up the way; and above all, if the very jaws of hell shall gape open the mouth wide after thee, know thou, my son, that all these things shall give thee experience, and shall be for thy good. The Son of Man hath descended below them all; art thou greater than he?

Therefore, hold on thy way, and the Priesthood shall remain with thee, for their bounds are set, they cannot pass. Thy days are known, and thy years shall not be numbered less; therefore, fear not what man can do, for God shall be with you forever and ever.

Now, brethren, I would suggest for the consideration of the conference, its being carefully and wisely understood by the council or conferences that our brethren scattered abroad, who understand the spirit of the gathering, that they fall into the places and refuge of safety that God shall open unto them, between Kirtland and Far West. Those from the east and from the west, and from far countries, let them fall in somewhere between those two boundaries, in the most safe and quiet places they can find; and let this be the present understanding, until God shall open a more effectual door for us for further considerations.

And again, we further suggest for the considerations of the Council, that there be no organization of large bodies upon common stock principles, in property, or of large companies of firms, until the Lord shall signify it in a proper manner, as it opens such a dreadful field for the avaricious, the indolent, and the corrupt hearted to prey upon the innocent and virtuous, and honest.

We have reason to believe that many things were introduced among the Saints before God had signified the times; and notwithstanding the principles and plans may have been good, yet aspiring men, or in other words, men who had not the substance of godliness about them, perhaps undertook to handle edged tools. Children, you know, are fond of tools, while they are not yet able to use them.

Time and experience, however, are the only safe remedies against such evils. There are many teachers, but, perhaps, not many fathers. There are times coming when God will signify many things which are expedient for the well-being of the Saints; but the times have not yet come, but will come, as fast as there can be found place and reception for them.

And again, we would suggest for your consideration the propriety of all the Saints gathering up a knowledge of all the facts and sufferings and abuses put upon them by the people of this state; and also of all the property and amount of damages which they have sustained, both of character and personal injuries, as well as real property; and also the names of all persons that have had a hand in their oppressions, as far as they can get hold of them and find them out; and perhaps a committee can be appointed to find out these things, and to take statements, and affidavits, and also to gather up the libelous publications that are afloat, and all that are in the magazines, and in the encyclopedias, and all the libelous histories that are published, and are writing, and by whom, and present the whole concatenation of diabolical rascality, and nefarious and murderous impositions that have been practiced upon this people, that we may not only publish to all the world, but present them to the heads of government in all their dark and hellish hue, as the last effort which is enjoined on us by our Heavenly Father, before we can fully and completely claim that promise which shall call Him forth from His hiding place, and also that the whole nation may be left without excuse before He can send forth the power of His mighty arm.

It is an imperative duty that we owe to God, to angels, with whom we shall be brought to stand, and also to ourselves, to our wives and children, who have been made to bow down with grief, sorrow, and care, under the most damning hand of murder, tyranny, and oppression, supported and urged on and upheld by the influence of that spirit which hath so strongly riveted the creeds of the fathers, who have inherited lies, upon the hearts of the children, and filled the world with confusion, and has been growing stronger and stronger, and is now the very main-spring of all corruption, and the whole earth groans under the weight of its iniquity.

It is an iron yoke, it is a strong band; they are the very hand-cuffs, and chains, and shackles, and fetters of hell.

Therefore it is an imperative duty that we owe, not only to our own wives and children, but to the widows and fatherless, whose husbands and fathers have been murdered under its iron hand; which dark and blackening deeds are enough to make hell itself shudder, and to stand aghast and pale, and the hands of the very devil to tremble and palsy. And also it is an imperative duty that we owe to all the rising generation, and to all the pure in heart, (for there are many yet on the earth among all sects, parties, denominations, who are blinded by the subtle craftiness of men, whereby they lie in wait to deceive, and who are only kept from the truth because they know not where to find it); therefore, that we should waste and wear out our lives in bringing to light all the hidden things of darkness, wherein we know them; and they are truly manifest from heaven.

These should then be attended to with great earnestness. Let no man count them as small things; for there is much which lieth in futurity, pertaining to the Saints, which depends upon these things. You know, brethren, that a very large ship is benefited very much by a very small helm in the time of a storm, by being kept workways with the wind and the waves.

Therefore, dearly beloved brethren, let us cheerfully do all things that lie in our power, and then may we stand still with the utmost assurance, to see the salvation of God, and for His arm to be revealed.

And again, I would further suggest the impropriety of the organization of bands or companies, by covenant or oaths, by penalties or secrecies; but let the time past of our experience and sufferings by the wickedness of Doctor Avard suffice and let our covenant be that of the Everlasting Covenant, as is contained in the Holy Writ and the things that God hath revealed unto us. Pure friendship always becomes weakened the very moment you undertake to make it stronger by penal oaths and secrecy.

Your humble servant or servants, intend from henceforth to disapprobate everything that is not in accordance with the fullness of the Gospel of Jesus Christ, and is not of a bold, and frank, and upright nature. They will not hold their peace-- as in times past when they see iniquity beginning to rear its head--for fear of traitors, or the consequences that shall follow by reproving those who creep in unawares, that they may get something with which to destroy the flock. We believe that the experience of the Saints in times past has been sufficient, that they will from henceforth be always ready to obey the truth without having men's persons in admiration because of advantage. It is expedient that we should be aware of such things; and we ought always to be aware of those prejudices which sometimes so strangely present themselves, and are so congenial to human nature, against our friends, neighbors, and brethren of the world, who choose to differ from us in opinion and in matters of faith. Our religion is between us and our God. Their religion is between them and their God.

There is a love from God that should be exercised toward those of our faith, who walk uprightly, which is peculiar to itself, but it is without prejudice; it also gives scope to the mind, which enables us to conduct ourselves with greater liberality towards all that are not of our faith, than what they exercise towards one another. These principles approximate nearer to the mind of God, because it is like God, or Godlike.

Here is a principle also, which we are bound to be exercised with, that is, in common with all men, such as governments, and laws, and regulations in the civil concerns of life. This principle guarantees to all parties, sects, and denominations, and classes of religion, equal, coherent, and indefeasible rights; they are things that pertain to this life; therefore all are alike interested; they make our responsibilities one towards another in matters of corruptible things, while the former principles do not destroy the latter, but bind us stronger, and make our responsibilities not only one to another, but unto God also. Hence we say, that the Constitution of the United States is a glorious standard; it is founded in the wisdom of God. It is a heavenly banner; it is to all those who are privileged with the sweets of its liberty, like the cooling shades and refreshing waters of a great rock in a thirsty and weary land. It is like a great tree under whose branches men from every clime can be shielded from the burning rays of the sun.

We, brethren, are deprived of the protection of its glorious principles, by the cruelty of the cruel, by those who only look for the time being, for pasturage like the beasts of the field, only to fill themselves; and forget that the "Mormons," as well as the Presbyterians, and those of every other class and description, have equal rights to partake of the fruits of the great tree of our national liberty. But notwithstanding we see what we see, and feel what we feel and know what we know, yet that fruit is no less precious and delicious to our taste; we cannot be weaned from the milk, neither can we be driven from the breast; neither will we deny our religion because of the hand of oppression; but we will hold on until death.

We say that God is true; that the Constitution of the United States is true; that the Bible is true; that the Book of Mormon is true; that the Book of Covenants is true; that Christ is true; that the ministering angels sent forth from God are true, and that we know that we have an house not made with hands eternal in the heavens, whose builder and maker is God; a consolation which our oppressors cannot feel, when fortune, or fate, shall lay its iron hand on them as it has on us. Now, we ask, what is man? Remember, brethren. that time and chance happen to all men.

We shall continue our reflections in our next.

We subscribe ourselves, your sincere friends and brethren in the bonds of the everlasting Gospel, prisoners of Jesus Christ, for the sake of the Gospel and the Saints.

We pronounce the blessings of heaven upon the heads of the Saints who seek to serve God with undivided hearts, in the name of Jesus Christ. Amen.

JOSEPH SMITH, JUN.,
HYRUM SMITH,
LYMAN WIGHT,
CALEB BALDWIN,
ALEXANDER McRAE

(Excerpts of the foregoing letter are considered scripture by Latter-day Saints.)

CONCLUSION:
...I LIE NOT

Like the Apostle Paul, Joseph Smith suffered for his faith. They were not mere advocates for their religion. They suffered for it. As a result of their actions, we can know they were sincere in what they said because of what they did. Or, more correctly, for what was done to them for the sake of their faith.

These three crises and Joseph's response to each are valuable examples of the universal Christian struggle to keep hope in hopeless conditions. Every Christian soul experiences trials of faith. We all would like to build mansions of faith, but often see them turned to wreckage and ruin. Throughout years of wreckage and ruin, Joseph never doubted God. He only doubted his ability to accomplish God's work.

After the founding of a church in 1830, Joseph lived 14 more years before he was killed. Those 14 years were filled with trouble, opposition and violence directed against him. Most of his problems were as a result of those who were members or "former" members of the newly founded church. When God's voice told him "you cannot always tell the wicked from the righteous" it foreshadowed the events of this book. (D&C 10:37.) He trusted in traitors.

Many competing religious institutions claim they were founded by, and are the rightful successors to the legacy of Joseph Smith. They all retain very little resemblance to the original Mormonism of Joseph.

The many churches of Mormonism descend from an original body whose leaders betrayed Joseph. They did not embrace God's priesthood. When their faith failed, they blamed Joseph. When they were caught in illegal and immoral behavior, they attributed their misdeeds to him. Ultimately it was disaffected Mormons who conspired in 1844 to surrender Joseph to the Carthage, Illinois mob that killed him. Former Mormon leaders stirred up anger, then participated with the mob when he was assassinated.

The American public has been more than willing to accept a version of Joseph Smith that was contrived by critics. Ironically it is the modern believers in Mormonism who attribute greater dishonesty and misconduct to him than did his enemies. There are hundreds of "Mormon" offshoots that claim Joseph as their founder. All of them claim to be the "one true church" but none of them have been faithful to the original.

When the largest congregation (the Latter-day Saints headquartered in Salt Lake City) embraced polygamy, they attributed their abominable practice to Joseph. That LDS claim has become increasingly doubtful over time. Brigham Young, rather than Joseph Smith, appears to have primary responsibility for the practice. Once Brigham Young and the largest Mormon following adopted polygamy, they generated written evidence to vindicate their claim plural wives is an essential component to Mormonism. The evidence they generated fills volumes. Young's and his associate's propaganda is all most historians need to lay blame onto Joseph for their practice. However, considering only Joseph's public statements, he rejected and condemned polygamy and considered it adulterous and sinful. Those he discovered were involved in the practice were brought before the high council and expelled from the church.

In 1852, when the LDS church announced their practice publicly, eight years after Joseph had been murdered, they began to write retrospective accounts, amass affidavits, and preach that Joseph originated the practice. If only the records that existed at the time of Joseph Smith's death on June 27,

Conclusion

1844 are considered, the "proof" that polygamy originated with Joseph Smith is missing, contradicted, or at best ambiguous. But LDS historians unflinchingly attribute the abominable practice to Joseph, making him a liar, hypocrite and deceiver in the process. They do what Sampson Avard, traitors and apostates did while Joseph lived: blame their misdeeds on Joseph Smith.

Latter-day Saint Mormons have their version and traditions. They are unwilling to rethink the behavior of their ancestors. Like several other Mormon sects, they consider themselves "the only true" believers on earth, and cannot be corrected. This book attempts to reintroduce Joseph Smith as a Christian thinker who faced the universal challenges of believing in Christ. Christians would like to live for Christ's sake, and follow His lead. Since all have fallen short of the glory of God, we are confronted by setbacks and discouraged by failure. Joseph provides a useful example of coping with Christian crises.

Although he believed himself a prophet, Joseph did not pretend to be anything more than a frail, error-prone man in need of God's grace and forgiveness. He admitted failings, even recording revelations from God condemning his sins and failures. One revelation to him declared, "how oft you have transgressed the commandments and the laws of God, and have gone on in the persuasions of men. For, behold, you should not have feared man more than God. Although men set at naught the counsels of God, and despise his word—Yet you should have been faithful; and he would have extended his arm and supported you against all the fiery darts of the adversary; and he would have been with you in every time of trouble." (D&C 3:6-8.)

Mormons treated Joseph Smith poorly while he was alive, and worse in rewriting his history. They abused him and continue to slander his memory with revisionist histories composed to vindicate sins celebrated as sacraments. Even the Mormons who profess to honor him, misuse his name and memory to prop up false, prideful claims to follow a religion they say he founded. Joseph declared to the Latter-day Saints in April 1844 (two months before he was murdered), "You don't know me; you never knew my heart." (*TPJS*, p. 361.) That audience and its descendants have been the primary custodians of Joseph Smith's legacy. They have produced libraries of Joseph Smith biographies. Their work has overwhelmed any attempt to tell the events accurately. This book attempts to allow Joseph to explain his heart in his own words. When allowed to speak for himself, he emerges as a different man than the character described by his critics, or the fictional account advocated by the Latter-day Saints.

The Latter-day Saint version of Joseph Smith is a wily, complex and deceitful caricature. They believe he was a smooth, two-faced hypocrite who said and did one thing in private and another in public. But the historical record upon which they base their reconstruction is filled with alterations and emendations to support Brigham Young's agenda. One writer described the conflict,

> The official *History of the Church of Jesus Christ of Latter-day Saints* was published in book form under the direction of the First Presidency in 1902. The introductory assurance that "no historical or doctrinal statement has been changed" is demonstrably wrong. Overshadowed by editorial censorship, hundreds of deletions, additions, and alterations, these seven volumes are not always reliable. ...The nineteenth-century propaganda mill was so adroit that few outside Brigham Young's inner circle were aware of the behind-the-scenes alterations so seamlessly stitched into church history. Charles Wesley

Conclusion

Wandell, an assistant church historian, was aghast at these emendations. Commenting on the many changes made in the historical work as it was being serialized in the *Deseret News*, Wandell noted in his diary: "I notice the interpolations because having been employed in the Historian's office at Navuoo by Doctor Richards, and employed, too, in 1845, in compiling this very autobiography, I know that after Joseph's death his memoir was 'doctored' to suit the new order of things, and this, too, by the direct order of Brigham Young to Doctor Richards and systematically by Richards." The Quorum of the Twelve, under Brigham Young's leadership, began altering the historical record shortly after Smith's death. Contrary to the introduction's claim, Smith did not author the *History of the Church*. At the time of his 1844 death, the narrative had been written up to 5 August 1838. (Richard S. Van Wagoner, *Sidney Rigdon: A Portrait of Religious Excess*, Signature Books (Salt Lake City, 1994), p. 322.)

Following Joseph's death, the separation and dispute over history first played out between The Church of Jesus Christ of Latter-day Saints (Salt Lake City) referred to as the "Brighamites" and The Reorganized Church of Jesus Christ of Latter Day Saints (Independence) referred to as the "Josephites." These two largest Mormon churches held opposing views of the history and character of Joseph Smith.

Brigham Young compelled his Brighamite faction to practice polygamy claiming it was Joseph's secret teaching. Joseph's widow, Emma Smith, and her sons, rejected polygamy and maintained that Joseph likewise condemned it. The Brighamites carefully amended historical records to support Brigham's view, and after practicing plural marriages for decades, also began to compile affidavits to attribute the practice to Joseph Smith. The Josephites were likewise careful to compose history, distancing Joseph from these claims.

A careful review of all available historical records leaves the issue more uncertain than either the LDS Church or LDS authors claim. On the LDS side, most recently a physician has compiled a three-volume history supporting the LDS view that Joseph Smith originated and practiced polygamy. That compilation comprehensively documents the historical record. It is surprising how little contemporaneous proof exists. In order to attribute responsibility for originating the practice, it is necessary to consider materials written after Joseph's death (by those who wanted it to be a required part of Mormonism). Second-, third- and fourth-hand accounts make Joseph responsible. The historical source material raises many questions about reliability.

The best documentary "proof" of Joseph Smith's involvement with polygamy is a single document. It is a revelation attributed to Joseph Smith first written on July 12, 1843. An original does not exist. The version that survives is internally inconsistent and third-hand. The dubious document is on display in the LDS Church History Museum in Salt Lake City. It has been enlarged and hung on the wall. The document is in the handwriting of Joseph Kingsbury, who purportedly copied it from another document written by William Clayton, who is the one who originally wrote it down as scribe to Joseph Smith. Clayton's document was composed, according to him, from what Joseph Smith dictated. So the only LDS document tying Joseph to their claims is an undated Kingsbury copy of a Clayton composition that is attributed to Joseph. The date Kingsbury produced his copy is not known. How accurately it mirrors Clayton's original is likewise unknown. What changes, if any, were inserted at Brigham

160

Conclusion

Young's direction are also unknown. This is a subject far too complex to treat fully in this book.

Ironically, the greatest source of misinformation and false claims against Joseph Smith comes from the LDS church and its polygamous splinter groups that claim him as founder. It is necessary for them to denigrate him in order to justify their own course of immoral misconduct.

The competing Mormon churches have interjected so many contradictions into the historical record that it is almost impossible to now reconstruct a faithful account of Joseph. Therefore, if the search is limited to what he said, rather than to what others have said about him, the record may still remain incomplete, but it speaks clearly. Joseph was a man of faith who encountered terrible failures trying to preach faith in God. But he never lost his hope for mankind, and charity toward his captors, accusers and betrayers. He was more concerned with encouraging virtue in others than in condemning those who failed him. What he wrote is consistent with the highest Christian ideals.

Joseph translated the *Book of Mormon*, but almost never used it in his writings, sermons, letters or private discussions. His primary text was the Bible. He had confidence in his own revelations because he saw them as harmonious with and prophesied by the Bible. Joseph's First Vision experience was a direct result of his belief in the New Testament scripture, James 1:5. When Christ first spoke to him, He used the language of Paul and Isaiah to foretell Joseph's mission. When the angel visited Joseph with news of a buried book written on gold plates, the angel's message quoted from *Bible* passages of Joel, Malachi, Acts and Isaiah. Many of the revelations Joseph received came while retranslating the Bible. He would encounter mysterious passages that provoked an inquiry to God. The great revelation on the afterlife (D&C 76) came as a result of reading John 5:29.

Joseph's greatest sermon, *The King Follett Discourse,* expounded *Bible* passages. Though not commonly thought of as a Bible-based preacher, Joseph's ministry was grounded in the *Bible* and his sermons expounded *Bible* meaning and interpretation.

The most controversial issue involving Joseph Smith was the publication of the *Book of Mormon.* It, however, begins and ends with Biblical materials quoted extensively. Early in the book chapters of Isaiah are set out, followed by a commentary focusing the meaning on events in the Americas. It makes Isaiah as relevant a prophet for the American gentiles as it was for the Twelve Tribes of Israel. At the end of the book, Christ visits the Nephites and preaches The Sermon on the Mount, then adding words of counsel and prophecy. The *Book of Mormon* borrows *Bible* language, meaning, and prophecy, and then adapts the message to an American setting.

Joseph believed in God's ability to bestow high priesthood. He wanted it for himself and others. His encounter with God and its accompanying power was not something he could transmit to his followers. Joseph composed *Lectures on Faith* to lay out the path for others to follow to obtain faith in God for themselves.

Joseph may not have built Zion, but he foresaw it, advocated it, and prophesied it would be built on the American continent. Because of his faith in mans' potential to reclaim faith in God, there is a chance for Zion. If the prophecies of the *Bible* are true, then there will be a last days Zion, as Joseph Smith confirmed.

Joseph Smith said an angel predicted his name would be "both good and evil spoken of." That has proven true. Joseph has been vilified and praised as the founder of Mormonism. More than eighty-four different religious sects claim him as their founder, The Church of Jesus Christ of Latter-day Saints headquartered in Salt Lake City, Utah is the largest and most

Conclusion

recognized. Sadly they are among those who speak "evil" of Joseph to justify their own traditions, wealth, influence and authority claims.

It is not only possible, but likely, that Joseph Smith will have greater influence in the future than in the past. His influence is more likely to be found outside the various Mormon sects, and to spread into the traditional Christian world. The religion advocated by Joseph Smith was very simple. It is described in few words in the *Book of Mormon*. Christ spoke these words to an audience in the Americas:

> And this is my doctrine, and it is the doctrine which the Father hath given unto me; and I bear record of the Father, and the Father beareth record of me, and the Holy Ghost beareth record of the Father and me; and I bear record that the Father commandeth all men, everywhere, to repent and believe in me. And whoso believeth in me, and is baptized, the same shall be saved; and they are they who shall inherit the kingdom of God. And whoso believeth not in me, and is not baptized, shall be damned. Verily, verily, I say unto you, that this is my doctrine, and I bear record of it from the Father; and whoso believeth in me believeth in the Father also; and unto him will the Father bear record of me, for he will visit him with fire and with the Holy Ghost. And thus will the Father bear record of me, and the Holy Ghost will bear record unto him of the Father and me; for the Father, and I, and the Holy Ghost are one. And again I say unto you, ye must repent, and become as a little child, and be baptized in my name, or ye can in nowise receive these things. And again I say unto you, ye must repent, and be baptized in

my name, and become as a little child, or ye can in nowise inherit the kingdom of God. Verily, verily, I say unto you, that this is my doctrine, and whoso buildeth upon this buildeth upon my rock, and the gates of hell shall not prevail against them. And whoso shall declare more or less than this, and establish it for my doctrine, the same cometh of evil, and is not built upon my rock; but he buildeth upon a sandy foundation, and the gates of hell stand open to receive such when the floods come and the winds beat upon them. (3 Ne. 11:32-40.)

Joseph Smith was killed in Carthage, Illinois by a mob of dissident Mormons and state militia. He was first wounded in a hail of gunfire through the door of a second-story room of the Carthage Jail, fell from a window to the ground below, and was then propped up against the prison well, where he was executed. In all four .50 caliber musket rounds ended his life. He was 38 ½ years old at his death. His life was short, difficult, controversial and filled with opposition. Despite his many challenges and defeats he never waivered in his confidence that God called him and gave him a work to do. He never doubted. Like Paul he suffered for his faith and accomplished more in his lifetime than do most believers.

Instead of any of the many biographies written by convert or critic, Joseph can best be understood by reading his words. You can take his measure and compose his story best by reading his responses to the three great crises explained in this book. Ask yourself, what sort of a man would write these words? The answer is, they came from a man without doubt.

164

Glossary

Aaronic Priesthood: Priestly authority believed by Mormons to automatically descend by lineage from Aaron to his descendants, but which can also be conferred by the laying on of hands upon gentiles who would otherwise not possess such authority. It has the right to perform outward ordinances, including baptism. This priesthood was conferred on Joseph Smith and Oliver Cowdery May 15, 1829 by the resurrected John the Baptist.

Avard, Sampson: (1800-1869) Mormon convert who resided in Missouri in 1838. As a member of the High Council, he organized a secret society of militant Mormons called "the Danites." This group initiated violence and retaliated for Missourian violence in the lead up to the Mormon War. Afrer Joseph Smith's arrest for treason, Avard testified in the Richmond court proceedings against Smith and attributed all the actions of the Danites to Smith. Avard's testimony was the chief reason the charge of treason was upheld in the preliminary hearing. Smith denounced Avard as a liar and perjurer and he was subsequently excommunicated. In later years he practiced medicine in Illinois.

Bishop Partridge: (1793-1840) Early Mormon convert and first bishop in the LDS church. Full name was Edward Partridge, but was often referred to by the title of "Bishop Partridge." Joseph Smith calls him "Bishop Partridge" in his letter written from Liberty Jail. When he died Joseph Smith attributed his early death to the stresses and persecution he endured in Missouri during the Mormon War.

Boggs, Lilburn: (1796-1860) Governor of Missouri from 1836 to 1840. He was the Governor when hostilities began between Mormons and residents of Missouri. As part of those events, he issued Executive Order 44 ("the Mormon Extermination Order") on October 27, 1838 calling on the forceful expulsion of Mormons (Latter-day Saints) from Missouri. An attempt to assassinate him while at home on May 6, 1842 was attributed by him to Orrin Porter Rockwell, bodyguard to Joseph Smith. Rockwell was arrested, but acquitted for the attempted murder. Boggs migrated to California in 1846 and lived there until his death.

Book of Commandments: A collection of revelations received by Joseph Smith published in 1833. Later expanded and superseded by a replacement volume titled The Doctrine and Covenants in 1835.

Book of Mormon: A volume of scripture Joseph Smith attributed to his translation of a set of metal plates. The plates were originally written by the aboriginal inhabitants of the Americas, then buried by the last contributing author approximately 421 a.d. The high point of the text is a post-resurrection visit of Jesus Christ to the Americas. Smith claimed the location of these buried plates was revealed to him by an angel, and the translation was accomplished by "the gift and power of God." The account was abridged by a man/prophet named "Mormon" and the book takes its name from him. Mormons accept the book as scripture.

Book of Moses: A book of scripture that Joseph Smith received by revelation as an inspired and expanded account of the book of Genesis in the *Bible*. It is believed to restore some of the missing materials which were originally in the account when composed by Moses. The text is included as part of *The Pearl of Great Price*.

Booth, Ezra: (1792-1873) Early Mormon convert who had been a Methodist preacher prior to his conversion. He was one of the men ordained to the Melchizedek priesthood in June 1831. His disappointment in Joseph Smith and Mormonism turned to hostility, and he renounced the religion. He authored a series of nine letters critical of Smith that were published in the Ohio Star beginning in November

1831. His complained of inconsistencies in Joseph Smith, the coerciveness of the religion, and the character weaknesses he saw in Smith. He later returned to preaching outside of Mormonism and denounced Smith and the *Book of Mormon*.

Community of Christ: A Mormon sect formed in 1860 by Joseph Smith's widow and eldest son, Joseph Smith III. The faith was originally named The Reorganized Church of Jesus Christ of Latter Day Saints, but in 2001 changed its name to "The Community of Christ." It is headquartered in Independence, Missouri and has approximately 250,000 members.

Corrill, John: (1794-1842) Mormon leader in Missouri and elected member of the Missouri State Legislature. He abandoned Mormonism in 1839 and published *A Brief History of the Church of Christ of Latter Day Saints (Commonly Called Mormons)*. It is 50 pages and still considered a valuable source of accurate information from the period. LDS Mormon historians are not uniformly willing to accept his telling of events, and some have regarded him as a bitter apostate with a colored view of the events. He assisted Bishop Partridge from 1831 to 1837. He turned against the church and its leaders during the Mormon War, and was instrumental in the surrender at Far West. He testified against Smith in the Richmond, Missouri court proceedings and was considered a traitor to the Mormons.

Cowdery, Oliver: (1806-1850) An itinerate school teacher who resided with the family of Joseph Smith, Sr. during the 1828-29 school year. He learned about the *Book of Mormon* from them. On April 5, 1829 he traveled to meet Joseph Smith, and the next day became the scribe who wrote down Joseph Smith's dictation of the translation of the **Book of Mormon**. The original manuscript of the **Book of Mormon** was primarily in Oliver Cowdery's handwriting. He would later claim to have seen the angel who delivered the plates to

Joseph Smith, and have heard the voice of God declaring the translation by Joseph Smith was correct. This testimony made him one of the Three Witnesses to the *Book of Mormon*. The testimony of the Three Witnesses is in the front of all editions of the published book. Cowdery also claimed to have been present with Joseph Smith on May 15, 1829 when the resurrected John the Baptist conferred Aaronic Priesthood upon them, giving them the authority to baptize. He was part of the church organized on April 6, 1830 and served as the "Second Elder" to the church. He, along with the other Three Witnesses (Martin Harris and David Whitmer) chose and ordained the first quorum of twelve apostles in 1835. Cowdery was excommunicated from the church in 1838 and left the faith for years. He returned and was rebaptized November 12, 1848 and died before he was able to relocate to Salt Lake City to rejoin the body of the Latter-day Saints.

"DHC": Documentary History of the Church. A seven-volume set published as the LDS church's official history. It is now being replaced by the *Joseph Smith Papers* project.

Doctrine and Covenants: A volume of scripture originally published in 1835 which superseded the Book of Commandments. It consisted of two sections: Doctrine: comprised of the Lectures on Faith. Covenants: Revelations, declarations and letters accepted as modern scripture.

Doniphan, Alexander: (1808-1887) Attorney, soldier and politician. He was a member of the Missouri Legislature and was a general in the Missouri State Militia when the Mormon War erupted in 1838. He was ordered to execute Joseph Smith but refused to carry out the order because he believed it was illegal. No disciplinary action was taken against him for his insubordination. He later acted as lawyer for Orrin Porter Rockwell when he was accused of attempted murder of Governor Lilburn Boggs. Doniphan later served in the Mexican-American War.

168

Glossary

Eight Witnesses: Eight men who testified they saw the metal plates on which the *Book of Mormon* was written. They testified that Joseph Smith showed the plates to them and they handled the pages that had been translated. The names of the men, along with their testimony, appear in the front of the *Book of Mormon*. Their names are Hyrum Smith (Joseph's brother), Joseph Smith, Sr. (Joseph's father), Samuel H. Smith (Joseph's brother), Jacob Whitmer, John Whitmer, Hiram Page, Christian Whitmer and Peter Whitmer.

Endowment: A ritual begun by Joseph Smith in Nauvoo, Illinois that was finalized by Brigham Young. It presents a symbolic account of the creation of the world including Adam and Eve. The ritual uses Adam and Eve to portray the mortal experience of every man and woman. The ritual takes initiates to converse with the Lord through a veil, preliminary to entering into His presence. The Lord questions the initiates to determine if they obeyed, sacrificed, were chaste, and consecrated their lives. After appropriate answers are given to the Lord, they are permitted to enter into His presence. A reduced version of the ceremony is still presented in LDS temples.

Enoch: Early patriarchal descendant, seventh generation from Adam. He is regarded by Mormons as the founder of the original City of Zion, which God took into heaven before the flood of Noah. He and his city are expected to return with Christ at the Second Coming, as referenced in the New Testament book of Jude 1:14.

Extermination Order: Executive Order No. 44 issued by Missouri Governor Lilburn Boggs on October 27, 1838 directing that Mormons be exterminated or driven from the State of Missouri. It stated in relevant part, "The Mormons must be treated as enemies, and must be exterminated or driven from the state if necessary for the public peace[.]" It was issued as part of the Mormon War of 1838 and was not rescinded by Missouri Governor Kit Bond until June 25, 1976.

Elder: Office in the church Joseph Smith organized April 6, 1830. This office had the right to preside, preach, teach, exhort and expound scripture. Elders were originally elected to their position by the body of members. The practice has since changed in the LDS Church to "calling" by a presiding authority, and sustaining (vote of approval) by a congregation preliminary to ordaining to the office. Joseph Smith was the First Elder in the church, Oliver Cowdery was the Second Elder.

Fable of the Bear and Two Friends: A story of two friends walking in the woods who promised to remain together if trouble overtook them. When a bear appeared, one friend abandoned the other and climbed a tree for his safety. The abandoned friend fell to the ground, held his breath and pretended to be dead when the bear approached. The bear sniffed about the ear of the fallen body, then moved on because it was uninterested in a dead body. His friend climbed down from the tree and asked what the bear said when it whispered to him. The abandoned friend replied that the bear told him to never trust a false friend who would abandon him at the sign of trouble.

Far West: A city in northwestern Missouri settled by Mormons after violence broke out in Independence, Missouri. It was the primary gathering place of Mormons from 1836-1838. Joseph Smith surrendered to the Missouri Militia at Far West in October 1838.

First Presidency: A presiding group of three men: a President, First Counselor and Second Counselor. Originally equal in authority with other groups, it has become the group with overall authority in Mormon sects, controlling all other bodies now considered inferior and subordinate to the First Presidency.

Glossary

Harris, Martin: (1783-1875) A benefactor who employed Joseph Smith to dig a well and cistern in 1824. Later he helped Joseph Smith financially while the *Book of Mormon* translation was underway. Before the translation was completed, he took a page with hieroglyphs to New York City to show them to Professor Charles Anthon of Columbia College. Harris said Anthon certified the characters were ancient and translated correctly, but when Harris explained they were from a metal book revealed by an angel, Anthon asked for his certificate back and destroyed it. Anthon offered to translate it, but Harris said part of the book was sealed. Anthon replied he could not read a sealed book. This incident was regarded by Smith and Mormons to fulfill a prophecy of Isaiah (Isa. 28:11-12). Harris later mortgaged his land to pay for the publication of the first edition. He was among the Three Witnesses to the *Book of Mormon* and his testimony appears in the beginning of the published volume.

Haun's Mill: The name of a small Mormon village in Missouri where a water-wheel mill owned by non-Mormon Jacob Haun was located. In 1838 approximately 30 Mormon families lived near there. During the Mormon War it was the location of a massacre when approximately 240 armed Missouri Militiamen, led by Col. William Jennings, killed at least 17 or 19 Mormons after they attempted to surrender. None of the Missouri Militia was killed.

Hinckle, George M.: (1801-1861) Early Mormon leader and member of the Far West Missouri High Council. During the Mormon War, he negotiated the surrender of church leaders without their knowledge, and misled Joseph Smith into leaving Far West to meet with the Militia leader Colonel Lucas. Smith believed it was negotiations, but instead he was captured by the Militia and spent six months imprisoned on charges of treason against the state. Hinckle was accused by Mormons of "deceit and treachery" because of the surrender of the church's leaders. He subsequently testified against Smith in court proceedings, and was excommunicated in 1839. In 1840 he formed another church called the Church of Jesus Christ, the Bride, the Lamb's Wife.

Joseph Smith Papers: A project presently underway to publish historical papers from the LDS church archives concerning Joseph Smith. Diaries and journals, histories, documents and revelations are included in volumes of the work. The project was funded by Mormon businessman Larry H. Miller, and the work is accomplished through the Church Historian's Office. The Church Historian's Office and editorial board interject explanations, footnotes and chapter summaries that give their view on the documents. Often the historical documents are contradicted by the interjections of the Church Historian's Office and editors.

Joseph Smith Translation: A project begun in 1830 and completed in 1833 in which Joseph Smith made corrections and additions to the King James Version of the *Bible*. It was called by Joseph Smith "the fullness of the scriptures" but was not published during his lifetime. Upon his death, it became the property of his widow, Emma Smith, who delivered it to the Reorganized Church of Jesus Christ of Latter Day Saints, led by their son, Joseph Smith III. It was published for the first time by that church in 1867.

Kirtland: Northeastern Ohio city that became the center of Mormon activities from 1831-1837. The site was chosen because many former Campbellite believers living in the area converted to Mormonism and provided the economic and population base for Mormon development. Joseph Smith relocated there in 1831 and remained until 1837, when he fled from the community because of hostility stemming from the banking failure of the Kirtland Safety Society. The first Mormon temple was constructed there.

Glossary

Kirtland Safety Society: Founded by Joseph Smith and originally planned as a bank. When the institution failed to secure a banking charter, it issued notes as an "anti-banking society" which still functioned as a bank. During a national banking crisis it failed and disgruntled investors blamed Joseph Smith for their losses. This led to apostasy by church members and hostility toward Joseph Smith and Sidney Rigdon. They fled Kirtland and were pursued for approximately 200 miles by angry former-Mormons intent on retaliation.

Latter-day Saints: The name of members of the church headquartered in Salt Lake City, Utah. It is the largest denomination claiming Joseph Smith as their founder, having an estimated 16 million members worldwide in 2016.

Lectures on Faith: A series of seven theological lectures delivered at the School of the Prophets. The lectures were incorporated into the LDS scriptures in 1835, later dropped in 1921.

Lucas, Samuel: (1799-1868) Major General of the Missouri Militia. He commanded the force that laid siege to Far West on October 31, 1838 and who obtained the surrender of Joseph Smith to end the siege. He established severe terms to stop hostilities, including surrender of Mormon leaders, surrender of Mormon arms, and transfer of all Mormon property to defray costs of the Militia. He commanded Joseph Smith be executed on November 1st but his subordinates did not carry out the order.

Melchizedek: A *Bible* figure who lived contemporaneous with Abraham and to whom Abraham paid tithes. He founded a city of peace which mirrored the city founded by Enoch. It is believed that his city, like Enoch's, was taken into heaven and its residents will return with the Second Coming of Christ as part of the "concourses of angels" who will return with Him. The *Book of Mormon* explains that his people were wicked, but through his preaching they repented and learned to live righteously. As a result, he was called the king of righteousness. Apostle Paul refers to him in his letter to the Hebrews.

Melchizedek Priesthood: A form of priesthood Joseph Smith believed was conferred by the voice of God upon a recipient. It did not descend by birth, but by the will of God. It holds the responsibility for administering spiritual blessings. First promised to Smith and Cowdery by John the Baptist, it was conferred by the voice of God for the first time at a conference in June 1831. Despite the evidence, the LDS church believes it was restored by Peter, James and John sometime between May 16-28, 1829. The LDS church claims to be able to transfer this authority by the laying on of hands, and therefore claims to have spread it throughout their adult male population. Until 1978, LDS Mormons refused to confer it on males of black African descent, but changed their policy at that time and now ordain "all worthy males."

Missouri War: A conflict which first began with a skirmish on August 6, 1838 at the county seat for Daviess County, Missouri when Mormons attempted to vote. Missouri residents were fearful of growing Mormon electoral power and attempted to prevent the election of Mormons and their sympathizers. Following the initial skirmish, conflict spread throughout the county. On September 20, 1838, about 150 armed Missourians demanded Mormons vacate their settlement at DeWitt within ten days. The tensions grew and Mormons retaliated on October 18th by expelling Missourians from Gallatin, Millport and Grindstone Fork; and plundering and burning houses in retaliation for the previous Mormon losses. Both sides finally organized into competing armies and fought the Battle of Crooked River, where church leader Apostle David Patten was one of the nine Mormons killed. Mormons regard him as a martyr to the faith. Alarmed at the growing scope of the conflict, Governor Lilburn Boggs issued an order to exterminate or drive Mormons from the state. In response, on October 29th, 250 men of the Missouri Militia attacked a Mormon settlement of 30 to 40 families at Haun's Mill and massacred 19 Mormons, including a 9 year old boy and elderly Revolutionary War veteran, whom they decapitated post-mortem. The war ended when Far West was under siege. Mormon leaders were inside the settlement and when they surrendered to state custody the Mormons surrendered arms and resigned to being expelled from Missouri.

Mormonite: The original nickname applied to those who believed in the *Book of Mormon* and followed Joseph Smith. It was intended as an insult.

Mormon War: See "Missouri War."

Nauvoo: The city organized by Mormons after the expulsion from Missouri. Originally named Commerce, the name "Nauvoo" was taken from Hebrew and meant "beautiful." It was given a generous endowment of municipal power by an act of the Illinois legislature incorporating the city. This allowed the residents to form a militia (the Nauvoo Legion) and a university (Nauvoo University). It grew rapidly and had a population larger than Chicago. That life abruptly changed in 1856 by the westward migration of Mormons.

New Jerusalem: A city of peace to be built in the Americas to fulfill prophecy. It is foretold in both the *Bible* and *Book of Mormon*, and is part of the Mormon beliefs about events that will precede the Second Coming of Christ. The location of the city is believed by most Mormons to be fixed in Independence, Missouri. From other revelations, Biblical prophecies, and teachings of Joseph Smith there is reason to doubt that location.

Packer, Boyd K.: (1924-2015) Member of the quorum of twelve apostles of the LDS church from 1970 until his death.

He served as president of the quorum of the twelve from 2008 until he died in 2015. He was regarded as an authoritarian leader who dealt harshly with Mormon intellectuals holding different views from the hierarchy. He was the moving force behind a number of excommunications of Mormons who wrote less than faith promoting accounts of LDS history. He is remembered for a talk given to LDS church educators in which he declared that "not all truth is useful" and therefore it should be suppressed if it did not promote LDS institutional interests.

Page, Hiram: (1800-1852) One of the Eight Witnesses to the Book of Mormon. He was in Jackson County, Missouri when hostilities erupted between Mormons and local residents. He was beaten severely on October 31, 1833. He remained faithful until the Mormon War and was excommunicated in 1838. He later was rebaptized by William McLellin into the Church of Christ (Whitmerite), which also included former Mormons David and John Whitmer.

Painsville Republican: Ohio newspaper published in Painsville, Geauga County. It was near the Mormon community of Kirtland, and became (and still remains) an important historical source of material when issues involving Mormons were covered in print. They published weekly from 1836-1841.

Pearl of Great Price: A volume of LDS scripture that includes The Book of Moses (part of the Joseph Smith Translation of the *Bible*), The Book of Abraham, The Joseph Smith History, Joseph Smith-Matthew (also part of the Joseph Smith Translation of the *Bible*), and the Articles of Faith (part of a letter composed by Joseph Smith and sent to John Wentworth, editor of the Chicago Democrat newspaper).

Peck, Reed: (1814-1894) Mormon negotiator with the Missouri Militia authorities who participated in misleading church leaders, including Joseph Smith, into surrender at Far West. He was disaffected from the Mormons, testified against Smith in the court proceedings in Richmond, Missouri, and later wrote an extended account of his Missouri experience referred to as the Reed Peck Manuscript. In his account he complains, "The very men who risked their lives at [Smith's] request to open a communication with the army are now branded as traitors." In his version, the lives of hundreds were saved because of the stratagem of surrendering the leaders.

Phelps, W.W.: (1792-1872) William Wines Phelps was an early Mormon leader. He printed the *Book of Commandments*, the predecessor to the *Doctrine and Covenants*. He wrote many LDS hymns still in use today. He defected from the church during the Mormon War, but remained in Far West when other dissenters fled. He later testified against Joseph Smith in the Richmond, Missouri court proceedings. He was excommunicated, rebaptized and reconciled with Joseph Smith before Joseph's death.

Pratt, Orson: (1811-1881) Early Mormon convert and one of the original members of the quorum of twelve apostles. Brother of Parley Pratt. He was a preacher and writer who performed missionary work in the eastern United States and British Isles. After Joseph Smith's death he followed Brigham Young, and became a polygamist. His wife, Sarah Pratt, divorced him, left Mormonism, and founded the Anti-Polygamy Society in Salt Lake City.

Pratt, Parley: (1807-1857) Former Campbellite preacher and early Mormon convert. He was baptized by Oliver Cowdery on September 1, 1830. He served as one of the first Mormon missionaries. Among his converts was fellow Campbellite minister Sidney Rigdon. He was an original member of the quorum of the twelve. Pratt was a prolific writer and composed two doctrinal works, *Voice of Warning* (1837) and

Key to the Science of Theology (1855) that influenced Mormon theology and are still in print. He followed Brigham Young, was a polygamist, and took as his twelfth wife, Eleanor, who was already married to Hector McLean. Pratt was murdered by McLean as retaliation for stealing his wife and taking his children. LDS Mormons view Pratt as a martyr to their faith.

Priest: An office in the Mormon movement that was established by a visit from John the Baptist with Joseph Smith and Oliver Cowdery May 15, 1829, prior to the organization of a church. Mormons believe priests have the authority to baptize as well as preach, teach, exhort and expound.

Reorganized Church of Jesus Christ of Latter Day Saints: A church organized by Joseph Smith's widow, Emma Smith and led by her son Joseph Smith III. It was comprised in large part of those who refused to follow Brigham Young westward after Joseph Smith's martyrdom. It is headquartered in Independence, Missouri and claims to have 250,000 members. In 2001 it changed its name to "The Community of Christ." Unlike the LDS, the sect never practiced polygamy, did not continue the practice of baptism for the dead, and reject some of the things considered scripture by LDS (Book of Abraham, revelation on plural wives, secret temple rites)

Richmond: City in western Missouri where Joseph Smith and other church leaders were imprisoned while awaiting a preliminary hearing for treason at the end of the Mormon War. The judge determined there was evidence of the crime and remanded Joseph Smith to the jail in Liberty, Missouri to be held until a trial on the merits.

Rigdon, Sidney: Charismatic Campbellite minister who believed in restoring a New Testament Christian Church before converting to Mormonism. Once converted, he became a confidant of Joseph Smith, assisted with the Joseph Smith Translation of the *Bible*, and was chosen as a member of the first presidency. Following Joseph Smith's death he opposed Brigham Young's claim to lead the church and was excommunicated in September 1844.

Rockwell, Orrin Porter: (1813-1878) Body guard to Joseph Smith and Brigham Young. He was a devoted and loyal friend to Joseph Smith, having joined in the Mormon religion at age 16. He was accused and acquitted of the attempted murder of Governor Lilburn Boggs. Later served as Deputy US Marshall in the Utah Territory. During his lifetime, he was considered as notorious as Marshalls Wyatt Earp and Pat Garrett. His nickname was "the destroying angel." He has become so much the subject of legends, mythology and history, that it is difficult to separate fact from fiction.

School of the Prophets: A theological training program where lectures were prepared to instruct members of the Mormon priesthood on how to acquire faith. The series of lectures were formalized and adopted as scripture titled Lectures on Faith and included in the 1835 canon.

Scripture: LDS Mormons have four volumes in their canon: The *Bible*, the *Book of Mormon*, the *Doctrine and Covenants* and *The Pearl of Great Price*. RLDS (Community of Christ) do not accept *The Pearl of Great Price* and also have different content for their version of the *Doctrine and Covenants*.

Seventy: A quorum established in 1835 whose primary responsibility was missionary work. The quorum was originally established to be equal in authority to the First Presidency and Quorum of the Twelve, and was comprised of seventy members. Following the death of Joseph Smith, the Seventy were considered inferior to the Quorum of the Twelve and First Presidency, and acquired administrative authority beyond missionary responsibility. They are considered part of the General Authorities of the LDS Church, and preside over all the church under the direction of the First Presidency and Twelve.

Smith, Don C.: (1816-1841) Don Carlos Smith was the youngest brother of Joseph Smith. He was an early Mormon convert, missionary, church leader, and later an editor of the *Times and Seasons* newspaper. He died of malaria in Nauvoo, Illinois. His daughter, Ina Coobrith, became the first poet laureate of California.

Smith, Emma: (1804-1879) Wife and widow of Joseph Smith, mother to Joseph Smith III. She was pregnant at the time Joseph Smith was slain, and delivered a son, David Hyrum Smith, in November 1844. Three years after Joseph Smith's death she remarried Lewis Bidamon. She denied Joseph Smith practiced polygamy and claimed it had been introduced by Brigham Young.

Smith, Hyrum: (1800-1844) Brother of Joseph Smith and one of the Eight Witnesses to the *Book of Mormon*. He served as a prophet, seer and revelator, and replaced his deceased father (Joseph Smith, Sr.) as Patriarch to the Church beginning in 1841. He was murdered with Joseph Smith when a mob attacked the prison where they were being held on June 27, 1844.

Smith, Joseph: (1805-1844) In a vision in 1820 he claimed to have been visited by God the Father and His Son Jesus Christ. Subsequently, he was visited by an angel who revealed the existence and location of a buried book written on metal plates that recorded a religious history of aboriginal American people. The account begins in Jerusalem at approximately 600 b.c., and follows the migration and struggles of the people for approximately a thousand years. The account includes a post-resurrection visit of Jesus Christ to the Americas. He was translator of the *Book of Mormon*, regarded as a prophet, seer and revelator by Mormons. More than 85 sects claim him as their founder. He founded a church April 6, 1830 in New York which was first called The Church of Christ, then The Church of Jesus Christ, then The Church of the Latter Day

Saints, and finally the Church of Jesus Christ of Latter Day Saints. As a church founder he was regarded as the First Elder, and later as the First President of the organization. He served as a Lieutenant General of the Navuoo Legion, Nauvoo City Alderman, later Nauvoo Mayor, and was a candidate for President of the United States at the time he was slain. He was taken prisoner in Missouri during the Mormon War of 1838. He was under arrest and the protection of the Illinois Governor in Carthage, Illinois when he was killed by a mob that attacked the prison on June 27, 1844. He was 38 ½ years old at the time of death. The *Smithsonian Magazine* ranked Joseph Smith as the most important religious figure in American history.

"TPJS": Teachings of the Prophet Joseph Smith, a book summarizing his writings and sermons.

Twelve Apostles: An ecclesiastical body formed in 1835. Members were originally chosen and ordained by the Three Witnesses to the *Book of Mormon*. This quorum was originally equal to the First Presidency (3 men), the Seventy (70 men) and High Councils (local bodies of 12 men), all of whom were considered to hold the keys over the church. Upon the death of Joseph Smith, his successor, Brigham Young, changed this and made this quorum superior to all others. They are considered to exclusively hold "all the keys" in the LDS church, and the senior (longest serving) member automatically becomes the president of the LDS church upon the death of his predecessor.

Three Witnesses: Oliver Cowdery, Martin Harris and David Whitmer. They claimed an angel showed to them the plates from which the *Book of Mormon* was translated. Their testimony is in the front of every published copy of the *Book of Mormon*. In 1835, they chose and ordained the first quorum of twelve apostles.

Times and Seasons: Mormon newspaper published in Nauvoo, Illinois from 1839-1846. From January 1842 until his death, Joseph Smith was editor of the newspaper. It is the original source for a number of historically significant Mormon events, talks and letters.

Whitlock, Harvey: (1809-1847) Early Mormon convert who settled in Missouri before hostilities began between Mormons and local residents. He was among those who received ordination at the June 1831 conference. When ordained he was possessed by an evil spirit, which was quickly cast out. David Whitmer pointed to his possession by an evil spirit as proof the ordinations were improper. Whitlock was excommunicated in 1835 and reinstated in 1836. He withdrew again in 1838.

Whitmer, David: (1805-1888) Early Mormon convert and one of the Three Witnesses to the *Book of Mormon*. He was baptized in June 1829 and was among those who formed the official organization in New York on April 6, 1830. He had conflicts with convert Sidney Rigdon and was disenchanted with the failure of the Kirtland Safety Society. He was excommunicated during the Missouri difficulties leading to the Mormon War and never reconciled with Joseph Smith. He wrote a retrospective account of Mormon history in 1881 titled *An Address to All Believers in Christ*. In it he recounts events from early Mormonism according to his recollection.

Whitmer, John: (1802-1878) Brother of David Whitmer and one of the Eight Witnesses to the *Book of Mormon*. Called to be the first Church Historian, when he was excommunicated in 1838 he took the church history with him. His departure in 1838 with the historical records forced Joseph Smith to begin a new church history.

Wight, Lyman: (1796-1858) A church and military leader for Mormons during the Mormon War. In June 1831, he was ordained by Joseph Smith to the Melchizedek priesthood, and in turn ordained 18 other men during the same conference. In 1841 he was ordained an apostle to replace the slain David W. Patten who had been killed in the Battle of Crooked River in Missouri. Following the death of Joseph Smith, he led a splinter group to Texas, where he was for a time the church president. He later joined the Reorganized Church of Jesus Christ of Latter Day Saints, headquartered in Independence, Missouri.

Young, Brigham: (1801-1877) Mormon apostle who assumed the leadership role held by Joseph Smith after Smith's martyrdom. At an election on August 8, 1844 the quorum of twelve apostles, led by Young, was elected to lead the church. Three years later Young held another election to become the church president. He led the relocation of Mormons to Salt Lake City, Utah, where he founded some 200 communities from the Canadian to the Mexican borders. He was a colonizer, Territorial Governor, polygamist and reputed to be the first multi-millionaire west of the Mississippi River.

Zion: A prophesied last-days community of saints to which the City of Enoch will return, and Christ will dwell. Originally expected by Mormons to be located in Independence, Missouri it was later relocated to Nauvoo, Illinois. Late in his life Joseph Smith changed the location to "the whole of North and South America" predicting it will cover the entire landmass at some point during the Millennial reign of Jesus Christ.

Zion's Camp: An armed Mormon expedition led by Joseph Smith in May and June of 1834. They traveled from Kirtland, Ohio to Clay County, Missouri in a failed attempt to regain land from which Mormons were expelled by Missourians. The expedition became only a "show of force" and was dis-banned before any actual armed conflict between Mormons and Missourians began. The Mormons remained dispossessed of their land, and were later removed entirely from Missouri by an order of Governor Lilburn Boggs.

Glossary

A Man Without Doubt

About the Cover: The cover artwork includes part of a public domain lithograph created in 1852 illustrating the martyrdom of Joseph Smith (printed by Nagal & Weingaertner, New York. It is based on a drawing of G.W. Fasel which was converted into a lithograph by C. G. Crehen). Joseph and his brother Hyrum were killed June 27, 1844 at Carthage, Illinois. He was wounded on the upper floor, fell from the window, and then dragged to the nearby well where he was killed. His brother died on the upper floor. Both brothers were shot four times with .50 cal. musket balls. The mob included Illinois militiamen, several of whom were Christian ministers. As the lithograph illustrates, the mob painted their faces black to conceal their identity. This book is published on the anniversary of Hyrum and Joseph Smith's death.

CPSIA information can be obtained
at www.ICGtesting.com
Printed in the USA
LVOW12s0009210716

497156LV00001B/111/P